MICHAEL FRAYN

Clockwise

A Screenplay

METHUEN · LONDON

A Methuen Paperback
First published in Great Britain in 1986
as a Methuen Paperback original
by Methuen London Ltd,
11 New Fetter Lane, London EC4P 4EE
Copyright ©1986 by Michael Frayn
Printed in Great Britain by
Richard Clay (The Chaucer Press) Ltd
Bungay, Suffolk

Frayn, Michael
   Clockwise.
   I. Title
   822'.914   PR6056.R3

ISBN 0 413 60290 7

CAUTION
All rights in this screenplay are strictly reserved
and application for performances etc.,
should be made to Fraser & Dunlop (Scripts) Ltd,
91 Regent Street, London W1. No performance
may be given unless a licence has been obtained.

Author's Note

This is an 'original screenplay' in the sense that the same author both had the idea and wrote the script (a primitive procedure which is still widely employed in the writing of books and plays, but which is not so common in the cinema). It is also the original screenplay in the sense that it is the version which the director actually shot, and which may have been cut or otherwise altered in the process of editing.

M.F.

Clockwise is a Michael Codron film, made by Moment Films Ltd, in association with THORN/EMI Screen Entertainment Ltd.

Cast in order of appearance:

BRIAN STIMPSON	John Cleese
GWENDA STIMPSON	Alison Steadman
WOMAN TEACHER	Penny Leatherbarrow
TED	Howard Lloyd-Lewis
MR JOLLY	Stephen Moore
STUDIOUS-LOOKING BOY	Mark Bunting
RUNNER	Robert Wilkinson
TICKET COLLECTOR	John Bardon
GLEN SCULLY	Mark Burdis
MANDY KOSTAKIS	Nadia Carina
PASSER BY	Dickie Arnold
PASSENGER ON TRAIN	Angus Mackay
PORTER	Peter Needham
TAXI DRIVER	Peter Lorenzelli
PAUL STIMPSON	Chip Sweeney
LAURA	Sharon Maiden
MRS TRELLIS	Joan Hickson
MRS WHEEL	Constance Chapman
MRS WAY	Ann Way
GIRL CASHIER – PETROL STATION	Ann-Marie Gwatkin
MANAGER OF PETROL STATION	Mohammed Ashiq
MRS WISELY	Pat Keen
MR WISELY	Geoffrey Hutchings
AUTHORITY 'A' PC	Geoffrey Greenhill
1st AUTHORITY 'B' PC	Richard Ridings
2nd AUTHORITY 'B' PC	Geoffrey Davion
MAN IN TELEPHONE BOX	Charles Bartholomew
MRS GARDEN	Sheila Keith
PAT GARDEN	Penelope Wilton
PAT'S SON	Christian Regan
AUTHORITY 'B' PC AT PHONE BOX	Alan Parnaby
TRACTOR DRIVER	Tony Haygarth
PRIOR	Michael Aldridge
LAUNDRY MONK	Ronald Sowton

LAUGHING MONK	Alan Granton
WOMAN OF LOW CHURCH APPEARANCE	Susan Field
1st AUTHORITY 'C' PC	Leslie Scofield
2nd AUTHORITY 'C' PC	Mike Glynn
1st HEADMASTER	Benjamin Whitrow
2nd HEADMASTER	Jeffrey Wickham
3rd HEADMASTER	Rupert Massey
4th HEADMASTER	Peter Cellier
5th HEADMASTER	John Rowe
6th HEADMASTER	Patrick Godfrey
7th HEADMASTER	David Conville
8th HEADMASTER	Nicholas le Prevost
9th HEADMASTER	Philip Voss
10th HEADMASTER	Geoffrey Palmer
DET SGT RICE	Nick Stringer
DET INSP LAUNDRYMAN	Peter Jonfield
COMPANIONS TO LAUNDRYMAN/RICE	{ Graeme Green Brian Portsmouth
PORSCHE DRIVER	Sidney Livingstone
MAN IN WOOD	Michael Percival

Production Designer Roger Murray-Leach
Editor Peter Boyle
Director of Photography John Coquillon, BSC
Music composed by George Fenton
Associate Producer Gregory Dark
Executive Producers Verity Lambert & Nat Cohen
Screenplay by Michael Frayn
Produced by Michael Codron
Directed by Christopher Morahan

1. Interior. Stimpson's House — Bedroom. Dawn.

Close up of digital alarm clock in darkness. The illuminated digits fill the entire frame. They show 6.59 and 55 seconds. The seconds display changes: 56 . . . 57 . . . 58 . . . 59 . . . The reading changes to 7.00, and the alarm sounds.

Cut to close up of Stimpson. He is sitting up in bed, already fully awake, switching the bedside light on and the alarm off.

STIMPSON (*quietly, voice over, but with his lips moving*). This is a historic moment.

Cut to close up of Gwenda, lying in bed beside him. She opens her eyes mistrustfully, turns her head very slightly towards Stimpson, then firmly closes them again, compresses her lips, and goes back to sleep. Cut to:

2. Interior. Stimpson's House. Bathroom. Dawn.

The shower-curtain, with the shower working behind it.

STIMPSON (*out of view, raising his voice above shower noise*). I stand before you today as your new Chairman . . .

The shower is turned off and the curtain pulled abruptly back, revealing Stimpson naked and wet.

. . . Something that few of us ever expected to see in our lifetime.

Cut to:

3. Interior. Stimpson's House. Bedroom. Morning.

Close up of Gwenda in bed in foreground, but turned away from Stimpson, who can be seen in the background, dressed and tying his tie in the mirror. The curtains have been opened, and the room is light. She opens her eyes, aware that Stimpson is in the room.

GWENDA (*irritated*). I *could* have gone with you. You *could* have taken me.

Cut to Stimpson at the mirror, with Gwenda in the background behind him.

STIMPSON (*voice over*). This is a historic moment. I stand before you today as your new Chairman . . .

Cut to Gwenda, as before.

GWENDA (*resentfully*). I wasn't going to come into the meeting. I don't know how I could put you off if I don't even come into the meeting.

Cut to Stimpson, at the mirror.

STIMPSON (*voice over*). We have come a long way together to be where we are today, and I cannot but feel deeply humble.

He has finished at the mirror. Pan with him as he crosses to the bed, where Gwenda is now sitting up, irritated at his failure to respond. He picks up his watch from the bedside table and straps it on.

GWENDA. I said how could I put you off, if I'm not there when you make the speech?

Pan with Stimpson as he turns and goes to the door. As he reaches it he becomes belatedly aware that she has spoken.

STIMPSON. What?

Cut to Gwenda, in bed.

GWENDA. I asked you a question.

Cut to Stimpson, at the bedroom door.

STIMPSON. Oh, sorry. (*He glances automatically at his watch.*) Seven-twenty.

He goes out of the room.

Cut to Gwenda, in bed. She turns away and lies down, deeply offended. Cut to:

4. Exterior. School playground. Day.

The playground of a mixed comprehensive school housed in modern buildings. It is just before the start of morning school in late September, and the playground is crowded.

Various shots of pupils messing around, playing, chatting, jeering at each other, etc. Pan up to:

Window of Headmaster's study. The neat regular lines of the window fill the frame, like the digital display of the alarm clock in Scene 1. One of the windows is open, and Stimpson can be seen inside, visibly watching the scene in the playground. Suddenly he picks up a pair of binoculars and looks through them.

Cut to a group of boys in the playground. Two boys are just beginning to torture a third. A fourth boy, one of the persecutors, glances upwards in the direction of the headmaster's study. It is evidently a habitual precaution. What he sees makes him shake the arms of the torturers. They glance up in their turn, and let their victim go. He glances up no less guiltily. Cut to: .

5. Exterior. School playground. Day.

Window of Headmaster's study. Stimpson lowers the binoculars, satisfied. Then he puts them to his eyes again, looking in a different direction. He picks up a microphone.

STIMPSON (*his voice hugely magnified by PA*). Right — Orridge, Popple, Patel.

Cut to Orridge, Popple, Patel. The first two are looking at a school atlas that Patel is holding, in the most law-abiding and studious way. They look up, surprised to be addressed in their innocence. The noise in the playground dies down.

STIMPSON (*out of view, over PA*). Nine-twenty.

Patel puts a hand to his chest to mean, What — us? Me? As he does so a number of photographs slide out from behind the atlas. He retrieves them quickly, glancing up in the direction of the headmaster's study.

Cut to:

6. Interior. Headmaster's study. Day.

Stimpson, standing near the open window. He lowers the binoculars and puts down the microphone. He resumes reading from a typescript in front of him, speaking at normal room volume, but with the attitude which suggests he is addressing the crowd in the playground outside.

STIMPSON. . . . cannot but feel deeply humble. Five years

ago, if I may be personal for a moment, a rather overawed headmaster of a rather obscure maintained comprehensive school . . .

The phone on his desk rings. He picks up the receiver.

(*Into phone.*) Stimpson . . .

He glances at his watch while the caller explains his business, then up at the clock on the wall. Pan to: clock. Its digital numerals show 8.49.

Cut to Stimpson, phone to his ear, still looking expectantly at the clock.

(*Into phone.*) No, 10.35 on Thursday. Or 12.10 Friday.

Cut to clock on wall. The time changes from 8.49 to 8.50. The school bell rings.

Cut to Stimpson, as before. He glances at his watch, then turns to look out of the window.

(*Into phone.*) Or we could say 11.10 on Friday week.

He takes the receiver away from his mouth and picks up the microphone.

(*Into microphone.*) Don't run! Sharon Seeds. Nine-twenty. (*Into phone, turning to make a note on a complex timetable covering the wall.*) Eleven-ten . . . Right. (*He puts the receiver down and speaks from his typescript again.*) . . . of a rather obscure maintained comprehensive school arrived at Annual Meeting for the first time, amazed to find himself invited to become one of your very select handful of Additional Members.

A knock at the door.

Come in . . . He listened to the headmasters of schools with great and glorious names . . . Come in . . . !

The door opens, and a Woman Teacher enters.

. . . great and glorious names . . .

WOMAN TEACHER. Headmaster . . .

STIMPSON. Eton and Winchester, Repton and Stowe . . .

WOMAN TEACHER. Am I taking 4H in G3 at 10.30?

STIMPSON. . . . as they expatiated upon a variety of weighty matters, and scarcely did our nervous new boy open his mouth.

WOMAN TEACHER. Sorry. This is your thing with all the posh schools?

STIMPSON. 4H in G3 at 10.30?

He taps the keys of a computer terminal on his desk. Ted, another teacher, puts his head round the open door.

TED. Two-fifteen. OK, Brian?

WOMAN TEACHER (*to Ted*). Joan says I'm taking 4H in G3 at 10.30. I thought I was taking 4J in J3 at 11.

STIMPSON. Peter Stiles is taking 4H in G3 at 10.30. (*To Ted.*) Right, Ted, 2.15.

TED. Slay them at the Conference, Brian. Tell all those upper-class ponces we're going to hang them from the lamp-posts by their old school ties.

STIMPSON. Right. Thank you, Ted.

Ted goes out.

(*To Woman Teacher.*) You're taking 4G in H3 at 10.35.

WOMAN TEACHER. Oh God. They should try having 4G at Harrow.

She goes out.

STIMPSON (*reads from typescript*). Well, that obscure comprehensive school was none other than Thomas Tompion, and that overawed new boy was none other than me. Little did he dream . . .

The school bell rings. Stimpson glances at his watch, then up at the clock on the wall.

Cut to clock. It shows 8.55.

Cut to Stimpson. He glances out of the window. Satisfied with the scene in the playground, he returns to his typescript.

Little did he cream that within a few short years he would be standing up here himself as the very first comprehensive school headmaster ever . . . (*His attention is distracted by something in the playground.*) . . . to become Chairman of the Headmasters' Conference! (*Into microphone.*) Clint!

7. Exterior. Playground. Day.

Clint, who is lumbering slowly across the empty playground, stops hopelessly at the sound of his name, and looks up towards the headmaster's study.

STIMPSON (*over PA*). Where do you think you're going, Clint? The Guinness Book of Records? Every day this term so far, isn't it, Clint?

Clint tries to remember.

Don't just stand there, Clint! Run!

Clint lumbers slowly away.

Nine-twenty, Clint. And come out from behind that door!

Clint stops, bewildered.

Not you. You!

Clint looks round. Pan to open door. Feet are visible underneath it. The feet move uncertainly.

Yes, you! I can see the smoke, you fool, I can see your feet!

Mr Jolly emerges from behind the door, holding a cigarette. He is one of the teachers — a wretched, smiling, hunted man.

Oh, it's you.

Mr Jolly gestures smiling apologies for his existence. Cut to:

8. Interior. School hall. Day.

The hall is full and the air is full of the murmer of its fullness. The pupils are all seated, waiting.

Cut to platform at front of hall.

The staff are assembled, also seated, also waiting. The lectern in the middle is unoccupied. One of the staff glances at her watch, then up towards the clock over the doors at the back.

Cut to close up of clock. It shows 8.59. It changes to 9.00. The school bell rings. Pan down to the doors as Stimpson sweeps in.

Cut to platform. The staff rise to their feet.

Cut to assembled pupils. They rise to their feet, and the

*murmer in the air falls to silence, as Stimpson sweeps up the
central aisle. Pan with him as he ascends the platform and
takes his place at the lectern. He gestures for the school to sit.*

Cut to point of view of assembled pupils. They sit.

*Cut to Stimpson on platform. He is entirely at home, in easy,
good-humoured command of his audience.*

STIMPSON. Right, now I've got some sad news for you all.
I'm going to be away today.

Discreet ironic cheer from the pupils, out of view.

I knew you'd be heartbroken. Right, now where am I
going? I'm going to the University of East Anglia, at
Norwich, in the fair county of Norfolk. And why am I
going there? I'm going there because that's where this
year's Annual Meeting of the Headmasters' Conference is
being held, and you can all feel rather proud of yourselves.

*Cut to pan along faces of pupils listening with dutiful
interest.*

Because they don't let just any old headmasters into the
Headmasters' Conference. Far from it. The Headmasters'
Conference is the organisation to which all the great
independent schools in this country belong. Places like
Eton and Harrow, Winchester and Westminster.

Cut to Stimpson.

The fee-paying schools. The *posh* schools that we all look
down our noses at . . .

*Cut to Ted, the male teacher seen earlier in Stimpson's
study, standing among the rest of the staff. He does not
react to this dig, but one of his colleagues glances at him
and suppresses a grin.*

(*Out of view.*) . . . and that we'd all send our children to if
only we'd got the money. They don't usually let in the
headmasters of common-or-garden comprehensive schools,
or schools like this one.

Cut to Stimpson.

So why, you ask, why did they let *me* in? I'll tell you why.
They let me in because you and I — all of us together —
have made Thomas Tompion one of the best schools in

the country.

A yelp of inappropriate nervous laughter, followed by a murmur of laughter at the laugh. Stimpson is not disconcerted in any way.

Right, then, but today — nine-twenty, Linda — today is an extra special occasion. Because today, today, I take over as Chairman. Chairman of the Headmasters' Conference. And I shall be the first Chairman in the whole of history, the whole of history, who is headmaster of an ordinary common-or-garden state comprehensive school. So it really is one for the Guinness Book of Records.

Cut to point of view of pupils. Pan slowly over them, showing local reaction to the references that follow.

(*Out of view.*) Right, now. So what am I going to tell them in my speech this afternoon? I'm going to tell them how we did it. I'm going to tell them how we all decided that we wanted a well-run, orderly school. A school where we all knew what we supposed to be doing, Jimmy Picken. A school where we all knew which room we were supposed to be doing it in — I'm not looking at you, Wendy Pillbrow, or you, Garry Bottoms. And what we were supposed to be doing it with, Debbie Jones. And above all — Clint Ayling and Dean Striver please note . . .

Cut to close up of Stimpson. He suddenly raised his voice from these good-humoured jabs to a parade-ground blast of enormous volume.

. . . when we supposed to be doing it!

Cut to clock at the back of the hall. It changes from 9.04 to 9.05.

Cut to Stimpson. His voice has returned to its normal level, as though it had never been raised.

Right. Hymn 397. He who would valiant be.

The sound of everyone rising to his feet. Stimpson waits. Silence. Stimpson turns to look out of frame. So do the rest of the staff. Pan to piano, in front of platform to one side. There is no one sitting at it.

Cut to Stimpson. A twitch of resigned impatience. He looks round for the missing pianist.

Cut to Mr Jolly. He comes squeezing hurriedly down the side-aisle, past the standing pupils, who turn to see who it is. Faint noises of derision. With apologetic smiles and gestures towards the Headmaster he sits hurriedly down at the piano, and plays the opening chord.

Cut to Stimpson. He compresses his lips, then launches with everyone else into the hymn: 'He who would valiant be, 'Gainst all disaster . . .' Dissolve to:

9. Interior. Corridor outside Headmaster's study. Day.

Pan with Mr Jolly, as he comes along the corridor, passing some twenty pupils who are lined up against the wall, among them Clint, Orridge, Popple, and Patel. Some are lounging defiantly, some look apprehensive or bored.

MR JOLLY. You here again, Gayle?

Gayle won't answer.

(*To Patel.*) What are you here for, Shyam?

PATEL (*insolently*). Don't know. What are you here for?

MR JOLLY. Oh, I'm just. I'm merely.

Mr Jolly passes on to the head of the queue, outside Stimpson's door. The first person in the queue is Gwenda, the second, a studious-looking boy.

Hello, Mrs Stimpson.

Gwenda nods.

Surprised to find you line up with the. What have you been?

GWENDA. What?

MR JOLLY (*humorously*). Did you overcook the? Or were you late getting him his?

GWENDA. Late?

She looks up at the clock on the wall. It shows 9.19. Mr Jolly smilingly gestures for her not to bother with his attempts to communicate. Commotion out of frame. Mr Jolly looks back down the queue.

Pan to far end of queue. Two boys are fighting.

Cut to Mr Jolly. He turns and looks up at the clock,

apprehensive for the boys who are fighting.

Pan up to clock. The 9.19 changes to 9.20. Pan back to Mr Jolly. He turns to look in the direction of the study door.

Pan to study door. It is flung open, and Stimpson emerges into the corridor. Standing right next to Gwenda and Mr Jolly he shouts down the corridor, using the same astonishingly loud voice that he produced in assembly.

STIMPSON. If you think 9.20 outside my study means 11.10 in the playground then you'll be back here at 9.20 every day until you learn to tell the time!

Absolute silence from the corridor. Stimpson continues to Gwenda at a normal conversational level.

I told you 9.50. The train's not till 10.25. (*To the studious-looking boy.*) What do *you* want?

STUDIOUS-LOOKING BOY. Please, sir, it's about starting Greek, sir.

STIMPSON (*good-humoured*). 9.20's not starting Greek. 9.20's not being driven to the railway station. (*To the next boy in the queue.*) What's 9.20?

NEXT BOY IN QUEUE. Executions, sir.

STIMPSON. Executions. (*To Mr Jolly.*) Mr Jolly . . .

Stimpson goes back into his study, followed by Mr Jolly. Cut to:

10. Interior. Headmaster's study. Day.

Stimpson crosses to the window and gazes out. Mr Jolly comes in and closes the door behind him.

STIMPSON. I used to be like you. Always late. Oh yes. Forever in the wrong place at the wrong time.

He picks up the binoculars and looks through them at something out of the window as he talks.

Pause.

MR. JOLLY. I know what you mean, but. I just thought I ought to come and. One or two things I ought to. One or two problems. One or two personal.

STIMPSON. I was like some miserable child wandering round
the school with his calculator in one hand and his gym
shoes in the other, and not the slightest idea where he's
supposed to be. (*Into microphone.*) G3, Leroy!

MR JOLLY. I know the feeling but.

STIMPSON (*to Mr Jolly*). We all go through it, John. We all
get lost.

MR JOLLY. I'm afraid I've got into, well. I've got into.

STIMPSON. Bed, John.

MR JOLLY. Oh no! No, no, no! Nothing like that! Well . . .

STIMPSON. Try getting out of it earlier in the morning.

MR JOLLY. Oh, Yes. But the thing is this.

STIMPSON. Because the first step to knowing *who* we are
is knowing *where* we are and *when* we are.

Cut to:

11. Exterior. School playground. Day.

*A grinning male sixth-former runs from one open door to
another with no clothes on. It is all over in a couple of
seconds. Cut to:*

12. Exterior. Classroom window. Day.

*Classroom window. Pupils inside react, laughing and cheering.
Cut to:*

13. Exterior. School playground. Day.

*Window of headmaster's study. Stimpson, standing with his
back to the open window, spins round, too late, to see what's
provoked the noise. Dissolve to:*

14. Exterior. Front of school. Day.

*A Ford Cortina comes out of the school drive. Pan with it
as it joins the traffic. Cut to:*

15. Exterior. Street near school/Interior. Cortina. Day.

Gwenda is driving; Stimpson is sitting next to her.

GWENDA. I could drive you there.

STIMPSON (*reassuringly*). The train doesn't go until 10.25.

GWENDA. You're ashamed of me, are you?

STIMPSON. You could go over to the hospital.

GWENDA. Don't tell me you're not allowed to take wives, because if you're the Chairman you are. *I* know that.

STIMPSON. You could take some of your old ladies out for a drive.

GWENDA. I don't have to come to the dinner, if that's what you're worrying about. I could go out and get a hamburger on my own.

STIMPSON (*voice over*). This is a historic moment. I stand before you today as your new Chairman . . .

GWENDA. I said I could go out and get a hamburger in McDonalds.

STIMPSON (*absently*). Good, good. And did Paul get off to school in time?

Cut to:

16. Exterior. Railway station approach. Day.

The station is a provincial terminus. Pan with the Cortina as it draws up outside the station.

Cut to Stimpson, getting out of the car with his overnight bag.

STIMPSON (*to Gwenda*). Right. So you'll find somewhere to park?

GWENDA. Park?

STIMPSON. Make sure the train's running. If it's not you'll have to drive me there.

He slams the door.

Cut to close up of Gwenda. Her mouth tightens in irritation as she puts the car into gear. Cut to:

17. Interior. Station. Day.

Close up of station clock. It is showing 10.19.

Cut to Stimpson. He is walking unhurriedly to the barrier, eyes on the clock. He glances at his watch, then offers his ticket to the Ticket Collector.

STIMPSON. Right. Norwich. On time today, are we?

TICKET COLLECTOR (*dourly*). On the left.

STIMPSON. Right.

But his attention is distracted by something over the Ticket Collector's shoulder.

TICKET COLLECTOR. On the left, governor. Train on the left.

STIMPSON (*in his terrible voice*). Glen Scully and Mandy Kostakis!

Cut to Passers by. They look round at Stimpson, surprised by the volume of sound, then turn to look in the same direction as him.

Pan to Glen Scully and Mandy Kostakis. They are two high punks who are preparing to take their photographs in an automatic portrait machine. They look round at the sound of their names.

Cut to Stimpson at the ticket barrier. The Ticket Collector continues impassive while Stimpson shouts over his shoulder.

Yes! Right! (*He Looks at his watch ominously.*) Tomorrow then! Nine-twenty!

Cut to Passers by. They look back and forth between Stimpson and his two pupils.

Cut to Glen Scully and Mandy Kostakis. They shamble away, muttering.

Cut to Stimpson and Ticket Collector.

(*To Ticket Collector, his attention still on pupils.*) Right.

TICKET COLLECTOR (*woodenly*). On the left, then.

STIMPSON. Right . . .

Focuses on the Ticket Collector, and offers his ticket for inspection for the second time.

Right?

TICKET COLLECTOR (*waving him through*). Right, right.

STIMPSON. Right.

He walks across to the train waiting on the right.

Cut to Glen Scully and Mandy Kostakis. They stop and look defiantly back.

GLEN SCULLY. Where's *he* off to, then?

MANDY KOSTAKIS (*looking at Departures Board*). Plymouth.

Cut to:

18. Interior. First class carriage. Day.

Stimpson sits down next to the window on right hand side of carriage. He opens his overnight bag and takes out the typescript of his speech. He begins to study the speech.

STIMPSON (*voice over*). This is a historic moment. I stand before you today as your new Chairman . . .

Cut to another Passenger, sitting diagonally opposite to him, next to the window on the left hand side of the train. He looks expressionlessly at Stimpson.

Cut to Stimpson. He is smiling to accompany the words of the speech.

(*Voice over*). . . . something that few of us ever expected to see in our lifetime.

He becomes conscious that he is being watched, and glances up. Cut to:

19. Interior. First class carriage/Exterior. Platform. Day.

Other Passenger. He looks away, out of his window, through which a Porter can be seen, slamming a door on the train opposite, and waiting to signal the off. Cut to:

20. Interior. First class carriage. Day.

Stimpson. He looks back at his typescript.

STIMPSON (*voice over*). . . . something that few of us ever expected to see in our lifetime.

He suddenly looks up again towards the left hand window. Cut to:

21. Interior. First class carriage/Exterior. Platform. Day.

Left hand window, with Porter beyond. The Porter has his arm raised, ready to signal.

Cut to:

22. Interior. First class carriage. Day.

Stimpson. He looks at his watch, a sudden doubt striking him.

STIMPSON. This *is* the train for Norwich?

  Cut to:

23. Interior. First class carriage/Exterior. Platform. Day.

Passenger, with the Porter outside the window.

PASSENGER. Plymouth.

  Cut to:

24. Interior. First class carriage. Day.

Stimpson. He jumps to his feet, throwing the typescript down on to the seat opposite him.

STIMPSON. Plymouth?

  Cut to:

25. Interior. First class carriage/Exterior. Platform. Day.

Passenger, with the Porter outside the window.

PASSENGER (*indicating other train*). That was Norwich on the left.

  He nods at the train visible outside the window.

26. Exterior. Platform. Day.

The Porter blows his whistle and drops his arm. The train opposite starts to move.

Cut to:

27. Interior. First class carriage. Day.

Stimpson. He gives a terrible groan of despair, runs up the aisle, runs back and picks up his overnight bag, and runs off again. Pan to a big close up of the typescript of the speech, lying where it was thrown down on the seat, and sticking up so that its first paragraph is visible: 'This is a historic moment.'

Cut to:

28. Exterior. Platform. Day.

Stimpson comes stumbling out of the Plymouth train, and runs across to train opposite.

STIMPSON. Wait! Stop!

He begins to run after a passing door.

Cut to:

29. Exterior. Platform. Day.

Passenger in Plymouth train. He turns, watching Stimpson with sombre expressionlessness.

Cut to:

30. Exterior. Platform. Day.

Stimpson, running along the platform after the door in the Norwich train. It is going too fast for him. He gives up, and turns back.

STIMPSON (*inappropriately*). Right . . .

31. Interior. Station. Day.

Barrier. The Ticket Collector is holding it closed. Gwenda approaches him.

GWENDA. The 10.25 to Norwich . . .

TICKET COLLECTOR. You've missed it.

GWENDA. It's on time? It is running?

TICKET COLLECTOR. It's run. It's gone. (*Nods at the departing train.*) That's it.

GWENDA. That's all right, then.

She turns and starts to walk away again.

Cut to:

32. Exterior. Platform. Day.

Stimpson. He is hurrying back along the platform.

STIMPSON (*sees Gwenda*). Gwenda!

>*He starts to run.*

>*Cut to:*

33. Exterior. First class carriage. Day.

Passenger in Plymouth train. He watches Stimpson expressionlessly.

Cut to:

34. Interior. Station. Day.

Barrier. Stimpson comes hurrying along the platform towards it.

STIMPSON (*to Ticket Collector, accusingly*). Can't you tell the difference between left and right?

TICKET COLLECTOR. You said Norwich!

STIMPSON. That's Plymouth!

TICKET COLLECTOR (*baffled*). You didn't want Norwich?

>*Stimpson, hurrying through the barrier to catch up with Gwenda, suddenly stops dead.*

STIMPSON. Speech!

TICKET COLLECTOR. Speech? What — now?

>*The Porter's whistle blows, out of view. The Ticket Collector closes the barrier. Stimpson opens it again and runs back towards the Plymouth train. The Ticket Collector turns to a Passer by who has stopped to watch.*

TICKET COLLECTOR. They've asked me some damn funny things, but no one's ever asked me to make a speech before.

>*Cut to:*

35. Exterior. Platform. Day.

Porter. He is waiting to close an open door on the Plymouth train as it slowly begins to move towards him. It is the door that Stimpson left open when he got off the train. Stimpson comes running into shot. Instead of closing the door, the Porter holds it open for Stimpson and walks along with it, trying to help Stimpson aboard.

PORTER. Try this one, then? Plymouth, this one.

> *Track with them as Stimpson evades him and overtakes him, waving him away, unable to articulate.*

> *Track with Stimpson as he runs on until he is level with the same Passenger as before.*

STIMPSON (*to the Passenger*). Speech! Speech!

> *He gestures hopelessly at the Passenger.*

36. Interior. First class carriage. Day.

The Passenger stares uncomprehendingly, expressionlessly back at him.

37. Exterior. Platform. Day.

The train begins to beat Stimpson. He stops, gasping for breath.

STIMPSON. Right . . .

> *He turns and starts to stumble back towards the barrier.*

> *Cut to:*

38. Interior. Station. Day.

Barrier. The Ticket Collector and the Passer by watch Stimpson approach.

TICKET COLLECTOR (*to Passer by*). He's back. (*To Stimpson.*) Want the speech before you go, do you?

STIMPSON (*in great haste*). Norwich!

TICKET COLLECTOR. My lords, ladies, and gentlemen . . .

STIMPSON. Next one to Norwich!

TICKET COLLECTOR. 2.47. Change at Peterborough.

> *Stimpson gives a cry of despair and hurries on towards the street.*

TICKET COLLECTOR (*to Passer by*). He didn't like it.

> *Cut to:*

39. Exterior. Station car park. Day.

Cortina. Gwenda is just getting into it. Pan to Stimpson. He is standing at the edge of the car park, looking wildly round. He spots what he is looking for, and starts to run towards it. Cut to Cortina. Close up of Gwenda through driver's window as she starts the engine, sighing heavily. The car moves out of frame.

Cut to Stimpson. He gives up at the sight of this and leans against a parked car in despair.

Cut to pay booth. The Cortina stops at the barrier and Gwenda offers her ticket to the Attendant.

Cut to Stimpson, leaning against parked car. Hope revives at the sight of the Cortina stopping.

STIMPSON (*in his huge voice*). Gwenda.

He starts to run again. Cut to Pay booth. Gwenda is sorting out her change.

STIMPSON (*out of view, faintly*). Wait!

She pays. The barrier rises.

Stop.

She drives off. The barrier descends just as Stimpson runs into frame. He collapses over it.

Cut to Cortina. It stops at the end of the exit road from the car park, and waits to turn right into the traffic on the road beyond.

Cut to pay booth. Stimpson, leaning across the barrier, heaves himself up at the sight of the car stopping, and sets off in pursuit again.

Cut to close up of Gwenda in the car, showing the back of her head and the mirror. She is looking left and right, but not into the mirror, in which the tiny figure of Stimpson can be seen approaching at the run. The traffic clears. She drives forward.

Cut to Exterior. Cortina, as it turns right into the main road. It clears shot, there is a moment's pause, and then Stimpson follows it, running, across the frame.

Cut to:

40. Exterior. Street in town. Day.

*Tracking shot of Cortina from in front, showing the car
moving slowly forwards in a queue of traffic, and, a long way
behind, the tiny figure of Stimpson, hurrying and waving and
giving up and hurrying on again.*

Cut to close up of traffic light. It changes to red.

*Cut to close up of Gwenda in the Cortina. She reacts to the
light, and stops.*

*Cut to Stimpson, supporting himself against a lamp-post
some way behind. A last flicker of hope revives at the sight of
the stopped traffic. Track with him as he runs forward. He
reaches the Cortina at the head of the queue, seizes the locked
handle of the nearside front door, bends down, and calls
her name. But only a faint croak comes out.*

*Cut to close up of Gwenda inside the car, seen from the
offside, with Stimpson outside the car beyond her. She is lost
in bitter thoughts. Hooting out of view, to which she does not
react, but which causes Stimpson to look up towards the
traffic light.*

*Cut to close up of traffic light. It shows red and yellow. It
changes to green.*

*Cut to Stimpson. He reacts to the changing light. With one
hand he shakes the locked door, with the bag in the other he
hammers on the roof of the car.*

*Cut to close up of Gwenda inside the car, with Stimpson
outside the car beyond her. The hooting from behind and the
thudding on the roof rouse her from her thoughts. She half
looks round, half sees some demented man trying to tear open
the nearside door, gives a gasp of alarm, and lets in the clutch
very fast.*

*Cut to Stimpson, outside the car, as it suddenly accelerates
away. He gazes after it.*

Dissolve to:

41. Exterior. Stimpson's house. Day.

*Pan taxi up to house in comfortable suburban street. It stops.
Stimpson jumps urgently out and fumbles with his money.*

TAXI DRIVER. Keep going, governor. It's never too late till the last moment's gone.

Stimpson turns to run into the house.

TAXI DRIVER. Just so long . . .

Stimpson has to turn back reluctantly at the raised voice.

TAXI DRIVER. Just so long as your wife hasn't taken the car.

Stimpson turns and runs towards the house. Taxi Driver puts the money in his pocket and drives off.

Cut to:

42. Exterior. Garage. Day.

Stimpson runs up, unlocks the garage door, drags it open and groans. He slams it shut. Pan with him as he runs back towards the street.

Cut to:

43. Exterior. Stimpson's house. Day.

Pavement outside. Stimpson runs into shot and sees the taxi, waiting to turn into the main road, a couple of hundred yards away. He wonders whether to run after it, thinks better of it, and runs back towards the house.

Cut to:

44. Exterior. Front door. Day.

Stimpson hurriedly unlocks it and hurls himself inside.

Cut to:

45. Interior. Stimpson's house — hall. Day.

Stimpson erupts through the front door.

STIMPSON. Gwenda!

He flings open all the doors that open off the hall, one after another.

STIMPSON. Oh, *no*!

He runs out of the house. Pan up to top of stairs, where Paul, a teenage boy in his pyjamas, is just appearing, and gazing sleepily down into the hall.

Cut to:

46. Exterior. Stimpson's house. Day.

Pavement outside. Stimpson runs into shot just in time to see the taxi turning into the main road and disappearing. He runs straight back towards the house.

Cut to:

47. Interior. Stimpson's house -- hall. Day.

Interior. Hall, with Paul at the top of the stairs. Stimpson runs in through the front door, without seeing Paul.

STIMPSON (*shouting, to himself*). Where the hell is she?

PAUL (*dozily*). Um . . .

Stimpson jumps.

STIMPSON. Oh, *you're* here. Where's Mum?

PAUL. Um . . .

STIMPSON. Don't tell me at the school.

PAUL. Um, yeah, I think she's . . .

STIMPSON. I *know* she was at the school, you idiot! Where'd she go after that? Don't say the station!

PAUL. Yeah, I think she said . . .

STIMPSON. God give me strength!

He runs out of the front door.

Cut to:

48. Exterior. Stimpson's house. Day.

Pavement outside. Stimpson runs into shot, and looks wildly up and down the road.

STIMPSON (*to himself*). Where is she *now*, then?

He runs back towards the house. Cut to:

49. Interior. Stimpson's house — hall. Day.

Interior. Hall, with Paul at the top of the stairs. Stimpson runs in through the front door.

STIMPSON. She's not at the hospital? She's not driving old ladies round the countryside?

PAUL. Dunno. She might have said . . .

STIMPSON. She's at the hospital!

He runs out of the front door. Paul turns slowly to go back to bed, then stops as Stimpson comes running back in again.

STIMPSON. Why aren't you at school?

PAUL. Um, well, I've got a . . .

STIMPSON. You've got a free. Of course! You've got a free! Only you *haven't* got a free!

PAUL. No, I've got a . . .

STIMPSON. You've got a *Study Period*!

He runs out of the front door again, slamming it behind him.

Cut to Paul, gazing sleepily after him.

PAUL. I've got a hangover.

Cut to:

50. Exterior. Suburban main road. Day.

Track with Stimpson as he hurries along, looking over his shoulder for taxis, and glancing at his watch. There is little traffic. He looks over his shoulder again, and runs out into the road, waving wildly.

STIMPSON. Taxi! Taxi!

A car is approaching with a sign on its roof. As it passes him it becomes clear that it is a chauffeur-driven Daimler, and that the sign on the roof is the civic coat of arms.

Continue track with Stimpson from behind as he returns to the pavement and hurries along as before, still looking back over his shoulder all the time. While he is looking back, a Morris 1100 pulls out of a driveway to a house ahead of him, and waits, blocking the pavement, for a chance to turn out into the road.

STIMPSON. Taxi!

His head turns to follow the taxi he has seen, and he begins to run. He runs into the 1100.

Cut to close up of Laura, the driver of the 1100. She is a quiet, demure girl of eighteen. She is staring open-mouthed at what has landed on the bonnet of her car. Pan to the bonnet, with Stimpson lying across it, stunned.

Cut to taxi. It brakes and stops fifty yards up the road. The Driver turns his head, and looks back through the rear window.

Cut to close up of Stimpson, lying across the car bonnet, still not able to move.

STIMPSON (*faintly*). Taxi . . .

Cut to Taxi. The driver turns his head back to face the front, the brake lights go off, and it continues on its way.

Cut to Exterior. 1100. Stimpson gets off the bonnet, very shaken. Laura gazes at him through the open driver's window, horrified.

LAURA. Please, sir, I'm terribly sorry, Mr Stimpson, sir.

STIMPSON (*focuses on her*). Laura! Laura . . .?

She gazes at him helplessly. He urgently tries to find the words he wants, and not to let her go.

Laura . . . ! Laura . . . ! Laura . . . !

LAURA. I'm sorry, Mr Stimpson. I've got a free.

STIMPSON. Right. Laura. Hospital!

Laura gives a little whimper of guilt and alarm. Stimpson hobbles round the car, holding his knee, and gets in beside her.

50A. Exterior. Suburban main road. Day.

The 1100 travelling. Cut to:

51. Interior. 1100/Exterior. Suburban road (2). Day.

Laura driving, with Stimpson beside her. Every now and then she casts little appalled glances at him as he talks.

STIMPSON. Right. Right. Not far out of your way. . . . It's not a free, Laura — it's a Study Period. Study Periods are not frees . . . This is your parents' car, is it, Laura?

LAURA. They don't mind.

STIMPSON. You've got A-levels this year, Laura, you can't afford to go driving round the district in Study Periods . . . You're a prefect — you should be setting an example . . . Right — left . . . left . . .

52. Exterior. Hospital car park. Day.

The hospital is a rambling, chaotic muddle of ancient buildings and pre-fabricated additions. The 1100 pulls into the car park and stops. Stimpson gets out.

STIMPSON. Right. Wait here . . . Do you mind waiting . . . ? I don't know where she goes . . .

He runs up to a sign with many arrows on it pointing to different wards. He runs right, then immediately thinks better of it and runs left instead. Pan with him as he runs towards the door of the left hand ward and disappears inside.

MRS TRELLIS (*out of view*). . . . So she said, 'Ellie, it's no use letting Lou have the sherry glasses — she won't appreciate them, she won't polish them, you know what she's like . . .'

Whip pan to discover the source of this voice — Gwenda, ushering three elderly women patients, in various stages of confusion and amnesia, Mrs Trellis, Mrs Wheel, and Mrs Way, out of the door of the right hand ward.

MRS TRELLIS. So I said, 'All right, I've no desire to burden anyone with possessions they don't want, that's not my intention and never has been.' So she naturally thought that if the sherry glasses weren't going to Lou they'd be going to Pam, but I thought to myself 'Wait a minute, Ellie . . .'

GWENDA. Keep moving, Mrs Trellis. Nearly there.

Pan with them as they pass the bonnet of the 1100.

MRS TRELLIS. I thought to myself, 'Hold on a minute, Ellie . . .'

MRS WHEEL. Are we going to the hospital?

GWENDA. We're at the hospital, Mrs Wheel. We're going for a little drive in the country.

MRS WAY. How lovely. Isn't that lovely?

Tighten, as they go out of frame, on to Laura, sitting in the 1100 with her hands on the wheel and her chin resting on her hands. She is gazing straight in front of her through the windscreen, unseeing, intent upon her own thoughts.

MRS TRELLIS (*out of view*). 'Not so fast, Ellie,' I thought. 'If Pam gets them she'll only give them to Babs, and we all know what *she'll* do with them . . .'

Cut to the Stimpsons' Cortina, parked very close to the 1100. Gwenda is opening the doors and embarking her passengers.

MRS WAY. Isn't this lovely!

MRS WHEEL. Are we going to the hospital?

GWENDA. Don't worry, Mrs Wheel. We'll get back to the hospital just as soon as we've had a little look at the country.

Cut to Stimpson. Pan with him as he emerges from the left hand ward and runs across to the right hand one.

Cut to Cortina. Pan with it as it pulls away from the parking-place, and passes in front of the door to the right hand ward. The voices inside the car become briefly audible.

MRS TRELLIS. Then I thought, 'Hold on — Millie's living in Majorca. What on earth is *she* going to do with two dozen sherry glasses . . . ?'

MRS WAY. Aren't we lucky people!

As the car clears frame Stimpson emerges from the door of the right hand ward. Pan back with him as he runs towards the 1100.

STIMPSON. She's gone! We've missed her!

He jumps into the car. Cut to:

53. Exterior. Hospital drive. Day.

The Cortina. It pauses briefly at the end of the hospital drive, then turns right into the main road. It is followed out by a large van. The large van is replaced by the 1100, waiting for a chance to pull out in its turn.

Cut to Interior. 1100.

Laura, driving, is looking at Stimpson, waiting for instructions. Stimpson is gazing unseeing in front of him, absorbed in some internal moral calculation.

LAURA. Which way, then?

Stimpson goes staring through the windscreen. A polite beep-beep of a hooter. Laura looks into the driving mirror.

LAURA. Left or right, Mr Stimpson?

STIMPSON. Laura . . .

She waits. Another beep-beep.

Laura, will you drive me to Norwich?

LAURA (*matter-of-fact*). OK. Where is it?

STIMPSON. It's vital, you see, Laura. I shouldn't ask you otherwise. It's the Headmasters' Conference! I am the first headmaster of a maintained comprehensive school — ever — in the whole of history — to become Chairman of the Headmasters' Conference!

LAURA. Just tell me where it is.

STIMPSON. It's not far, Not all that far. Not too far.

LAURA. I mean, left or right?

A more determined hooting from behind.

STIMPSON. Oh, right . . . Left . . . Right.

Cut to Exterior. 1100. It makes an undecided S-bend out on to the main road — right, then back towards the left, then right again.

Dissolve to:

54. Exterior. Service station. Day.

Pan with the 1100 as it pulls of the road and draws up at the pumps. Cut to Interior 1100.

Stimpson is consulting a road atlas.

STIMPSON (*uneasily*). A hundred and sixty-three miles.

LAURA (*unconcerned*). Right.

STIMPSON (*conscience-stricken*). We'll have to ring your Mum . . . (*Looks towards kiosk*.) They've got a phone here . . . I'd better talk to her myself.

LAURA. I'll do it.

She opens the door, and starts to get out.

STIMPSON. I mean, not if she's the slightest bit worried about it, Laura . . . I'll pay for the petrol, of course . . .

She slams the door. Stimpson gazes anxiously after her. Then he resigns himself, and gets out of the car.

Cut to Exterior. 1100. Stimpson gets out and starts filling the car with petrol. He looks anxiously across in Laura's direction.

Cut to payphone. Laura is holding the receiver. She gets through, pushes the money in, and asks to speak to someone. Her words, at this distance, are completely inaudible.

Cut to Exterior. 1100. Stimpson is putting the petrol in, and gazing at Laura.

STIMPSON (*voice over*). This is a historic moment. We are going a long way, we have come a long way, we are going 163 miles . . .

Cut to payphone. Laura is speaking very earnestly into the receiver.

STIMPSON (*voice over*). Five hours ago, if I may be personal for a moment, I was feeling deeply historic.

Cut to Exterior. 1100. Stimpson, still putting petrol in the car and gazing absently in the direction of Laura.

STIMPSON (*voice over*). Five years ago, if I may be historic for a moment, I was feeling deeply humble . . .

Another voice, speaking out of view, becomes audible. Stimpson, absorbed in his own thoughts, pays no attention to it.

MRS TRELLIS (*out of view*). Now the liqueur glasses came to me from my mother, so naturally Jeannie has always had her eye on them . . .

Pan to discover the source of this voice — the Stimpsons'

*Cortina, standing in the next bay along. Its driver's window
is lowered. Gwenda, lost in thought, is filling the car
with petrol.*

MRS TRELLIS (*out of view*). Every time she comes to the
house she makes some little remark — 'Oh, Ellie,' she goes,
'it must take you ages to dust all your glasses. I don't know
how you do it. I'm sure *I* shouldn't like to have all those
glasses to dust . . .'

*Gwenda hangs up the nozzle and gets back into the driver's
seat of the car.*

*Cut to Interior. Cortina. Mrs Way is sitting in the front
passenger's seat. Mrs Trellis is sitting in the back with
Mrs Wheel. She continues her narrative without a pause,
while Gwenda picks up her handbag.*

MRS TRELLIS. She goes on and on about those glasses! Never
stops! I sometimes wonder if she ever thinks about
anything else! She certainly never *talks* about anything else!

*Gwenda goes to get out of the car again, then freezes at the
sight of something outside.*

*Cut to Gwenda's point of view of Stimpson filling the 1100
at the next bay.*

MRS TRELLIS (*out of view*). I never say a word, of course —
I'm not much of a talker — though there's plenty I could
say if I wanted to . . .

*Cut to Interior. Cortina. Gwenda is staring out of the
window in Stimpson's direction. She turns as if she is going
to tell Mrs Way what has happened. Mrs Trellis continues
regardless.*

MRS TRELLIS. . . . Like the clock — that went to her — not
that she has ever wound it, not that she has ever so much as
looked at it from that day to this . . .

*Gwenda thinks better of saying anything to Mrs Way, and
turns to get out of the car. But once again she freezes.*

*Cut to Exterior. 1100. Stimpson hangs up the nozzle of the
petrol pump. Pan with him as he walks over to the kiosk
to pay. He meets Laura, on her way back from the phone.*

STIMPSON (*anxiously*). What did she say?

LAURA. Oh, it's OK.

STIMPSON. Really? I feel very bad about this Laura. What are you missing? You're missing double biology!

LAURA. I don't mind.

STIMPSON. You should mind, Laura! You've got A-levels, and I'm taking you out of a double biology! Laura, you're going to discover that life is full of the most terrible moral choices!

Cut to Interior. Cortina. Close up of Gwenda, staring through the open window.

MRS TRELLIS (*out of view*). . . . She's got rooms in that house so filled with things you can't open the door. She doesn't know what she's got herself! She's never going to sort it out . . .

Cut to Gwenda's point of view of Stimpson and Laura. Stimpson is inaudibly agonising about whether he is morally entitled to waste his pupil's day. Laura is smiling up at him, inaudibly reassuring him.

. . . In fact I said to her, 'You know what's going to happen, don't you — someone else is going to have to sort this lot out after you've gone, and it won't be Dibs and it won't be Lou, oh no, it'll be me . . .'

Cut to Interior. Cortina. Close up of Gwenda. She looks away, as if not believing what she has seen, then looks back.

But she never pays the slightest attention to what anyone says! I don't know why I waste my breath . . .

Cut to Gwenda's point of view of Stimpson and Laura. A decision has been reached. They get into the 1100 and drive off.

. . . I can tell you she's got a clock in there that came from Mother, it's worth every penny of a hundred pounds, and I know for a fact that it has never been wound from that day to this . . .

Cut to Interior. Cortina. Gwenda watches the 1100 depart.

. . . So when she was in the house the other day what do I see? She's eyeing the sherry glasses!

Gwenda turns to Mrs Way.

GWENDA (*still stunned*). Laura Wisely! She lives down the road! She's one of his pupils!

MRS WAY. How lovely.

GWENDA. But I saw the train leave!

MRS WAY. Isn't that lovely.

   Cut to:

55. Interior. Service station kiosk. Day.

Kiosk. Girl cashier at cash desk, and Pakistani Manager.

CASHIER. Hey, that bloke with the girl — did they pay? They didn't pay! They never paid!

MANAGER (*picks up the phone*). Blue 1100, was it? Did you get the number?

   But the Cashier is gazing out at the forecourt, open-mouthed.

Number! Number! I must tell them the number!

CASHIER. I don't believe this! There goes another one!

   Cut to:

56. Exterior. Service station. Day.

Exterior. Cortina. Pan with it as it moves off, with Gwenda visible through the window, still looking poleaxed.

MRS TRELLIS (*still faintly audible*). . . . You know what she's like — she'll never so much as dust them. . .

   Cut to:

57. Exterior. Busy rural main road. Day.

Exterior. 1100. Track with it in traffic on busy rural main road.

Cut to:

58. Exterior. Busy rural main road/Interior 1100.

Interior. 1100. Laura, driving, takes her eyes off the road for a moment and glances across at Stimpson beside her. He is lost in his anxieties. She looks front again.

LAURA. Don't worry. It's OK. Honestly!

STIMPSON (*voice over*). If Thomas Tompion is a success story, if it is a school sought after by parents who live many leagues outside our catchment area, it is because we insist upon certain traditional standards . . .

He becomes retrospectively aware that Laura has spoken.

STIMPSON (*absently*). Speech. It's on the train.

Laura glances at Stimpson again, not understanding, but not expecting to understand.

(*Voice over.*) I should like at this point, if I may, before I pass on to other matters, to pause for . . . Three hours. 160 miles in three hours . . . To pause for . . . say 3 and a half hours. 3 and a half into 160 . . .

LAURA (*reassuringly*). It's a good thing, actually. If you hadn't come along I might not be here now.

She laughs. He smiles automatically, without hearing.

STIMPSON (*voice over*). To pause for a moment to sound a note of warning. The one traditional standard that we can all comprehend, from monarch to crossing-sweeper, from Classical Sixth to Remedial Reading Group, is *time*.

LAURA. I had this great row with this bloke. I ran back to the house and I saw the car-keys and I thought, Right!

STIMPSON (*voice over*). We all understand, I think, that lateness is a discourtesy to others. What is sometimes forgotten these days is that it is 3 and a half into 160.

LAURA. I don't know where I was going. I don't know what I was going to do. I probably wouldn't be here now!

She laughs. He smiles vaguely.

STIMPSON (*to Laura*). I suppose not. (*Voice over.*) Is that it is an attack upon the whole social order. More than that . . . (*Aloud, dismayed.*) It's about fifty miles an hour!

LAURA. He didn't like it when I told him I was driving to Norwich with someone. 'Who?' he said. 'Who? Who?' He's so jealous.

STIMPSON (*to Laura, as he realises what she has said*). Told him you were driving to Norwich? Told who you were driving to Norwich?

LAURA. This bloke. (*She looks at Stimpson.*) I couldn't ring *Mum*! She'd have gone mad!

STIMPSON (*looks at his watch*). We can't stop again! (*He presses morally agonised hands to his eyes, then takes them away sharply.*) And I never paid for the petrol!

Cut to:

59. Exterior. Laura's house. Day.

Exterior. Pavement outside, where Stimpson first collided with Laura. A battered van pulls up, and Mr Jolly gets out. Pan with him as he walks up to the front door and bangs on the knocker. The door is opened at once by Mrs Wisely, who is holding a telephone receiver to her ear.

MR JOLLY. Mrs Wisely?

MRS WISELY. Police?

MR JOLLY. No, no. Jolly. Mr Jolly. I just wondered if Laura was. Are you Laura's? (*Alarmed.*) Police?

MRS WISELY. Laura's at school, dear. I'm on the phone. The car's been stolen! (*Into phone.*) No, it's not the police . . .

She beckons Mr Jolly in as she talks.

60. Interior. Laura's house. Day.

Interior. Hall. Mr Jolly hangs about awkwardly in the doorway as Mrs Wisely talks.

MRS WISELY (*into phone*). . . . . It's someone for Laura. (*To Mr Jolly.*) My husband. He's beside himself! (*Into phone.*) Well, you'll have to come back and speak to them, give them a description — is it a Morris or is it an 1100? *I* don't know . . . (*To Mr Jolly.*) He's in such a state, he doesn't know what he's doing, he lives for that car . . . It was standing outside in the drive . . . ! He goes to pieces . . . Is it about the anti-nuclear, dear?

MR JOLLY. No, no. It's just that Laura's not at. I don't want to alarm you but. I thought I ought to just.

MRS WISELY (*into phone*). Laura! She's disappeared! No one knows where she is . . . ! No, he's just said — he's here now

— he's just told me . . . ! (*To Mr Jolly.*) Who *are* you?

MR JOLLY. I'm well, one of the staff at the.

MRS WISELY (*into phone*). He's one of the staff at the . . . !

MR JOLLY. I'm, you know, the music.

MRS WISELY (*into phone*). He's the music! (*To Mr Jolly.*) He's coming home. (*Into phone.*) You're coming home, then . . . ? (*To Mr Jolly.*) He's coming home. (*Puts receiver down.*) He doesn't know what he's doing. He's going to do someone an injury. And you've no idea where she is?

MR JOLLY. Well, does she have any relations or, you know, I just wondered if she had any sort of, well, in Norwich?

Cut to:

61. Exterior. Laura's house. Day.

Exterior. Pavement outside. The Cortina pulls up behind Mr Jolly's van, and Gwenda gets out.

MRS WHEEL (*out of view, from inside car*). Is this the hospital?

GWENDA (*distractedly*). No. Just wait there. Don't move.

Gwenda goes out of frame towards the house. The passenger door opens, and Mrs Way gets out.

MRS WAY. Oh, doesn't this make a change!

Cut to Exterior. Front door. Gwenda knocks.

62. Interior/Exterior. Laura's house. Day.

The front door is at once opened by Mrs Wisely.

MRS WISELY. Oh, no it's not, it's Mrs — isn't it Mrs Stimpson?

GWENDA. I'm sorry — I just wondered if . . .

MRS WISELY. Laura's disappeared!

GWENDA (*her worst fears confirmed*). She didn't tell you she was going?

MRS WISELY. Not a word! And the car's been stolen!

GWENDA. I'm so sorry, Mrs Wisely! I'm so sorry!

MRS WISELY. We're waiting for the police! My husband's

out of his mind with worry! (*She drags the reluctant Mr Jolly out into view.*) *He* says she's in Norwich!

GWENDA. Yes.

MR JOLLY. I just somehow thought perhaps. Hello, Mrs Stimpson. I just somehow wondered if.

GWENDA. Of course. Everyone knows except me.

MRS WISELY. Norwich! What can she be doing in Norwich?

GWENDA. I'll tell you what she's doing in Norwich. (*Very distressed.*) She's going to the Annual Meeting of the Headmasters' Conference!

MRS WISELY. Oh, *no*!

MR JOLLY. You mean?

GWENDA. Yes!

MR JOLLY. You don't mean?

GWENDA. Of course! He wouldn't take *me*! I said I'd sit in the hotel — I'd eat in McDonalds — but oh, no, because he's taking *her*!

MRS WISELY. She said it was cello! Every evening. I knew it wasn't cello!

GWENDA. A schoolgirl! A child!

MRS WISELY. She's got her A-levels!

Mrs Way appears at the edge of the group.

MRS WAY. Oh, look, a little family party! Isn't that nice?

MR JOLLY. I think I'd better. I think I must be.

He departs. No one pays any attention.

GWENDA. I haven't said anything about his work, work, work. I haven't said anything about his everlasting Conservative meetings. But I'm not going to put up with this!

MRS WISELY. Her father'll kill her!

MRS WAY. Can we see over the house? Is it open today?

Cut to:

63. Exterior. Laura's house. Day.

Exterior. Pavement outside.

Mr Jolly is just opening the door of his van when he is accosted by Mrs Wheel.

MRS WHEEL. Which one's the hospital?

MR JOLLY. The hospital? I think it's (*Points down the road.*) Along the bypass and.

He gets into the van. Mrs Wheel starts off towards the hospital.

Cut to Mr Wisely, on his motor-cycle. Pan with him as he approaches his house. The motor-cycle is light and quiet. Mr Wisely is heavy and quiet — a non-committal, phlegmatic man, thickly wrapped in motor-cycling gear. He stops, and turns to watch Mr Jolly's van making an erratic departure at speed. He continues into his driveway, where he turns again to watch Gwenda coming out, propelling Mrs Way in front of her. Pan with Gwenda and Mrs Way.

GWENDA. Get in the car. I told you to stay in the car.

MRS WAY (*delighted and appreciative*). What a day! Where next?

GWENDA. Norwich.

She opens the door of the Cortina, pushes Mrs Way unceremoniously in.

MRS TRELLIS (*starts up, out of view*). Yes, so she says, 'What's happened to Mother's blue teapot . . . ?'

GWENDA. Where's the other one?

She looks round impatiently.

Cut to Exterior. Front door. Mrs Wisely has come out to meet Mr Wisely. She is pulling on an inexpensive fur coat.

MRS WISELY. She's in Norwich! She's at a conference of headmasters! With the headmaster. His wife's beside herself! And what about her A-levels? We've got to find her, Ted, you've got to talk to her! Get the car out! The car's been stolen! She's taken the car! She can't drive!

Cut to Exterior. Pavement outside. Gwenda is looking anxiously up and down the road. A police panda car pulls up in front of her and the Constable driving it addresses her through the open window.

CONSTABLE. Mrs Wisely? Stolen car?

GWENDA (*indicates the house*). There. There.

Mrs Wheel gets out of the other side of the panda car.

MRS WHEEL (*to Gwenda*). There?

GWENDA (*impatiently, indicating her Cortina*). Here. Here.

Cut to Exterior. Driveway. Pan with the motor-cycle as it pulls out of the drive and stops at the kerb. Mr Wisely is on the front, with Mrs Wisely on the pillion, wrapped unsuitably in her fur coat.

MRS WISELY. Now keep calm. Don't go mad.

Mr Wisely pauses an instant at the kerb to look up and down the road.

What are you waiting for?

The motor-cycle pulls out of frame into the road, just as the Constable walks into frame. He stops and watches the motor-cycle go, then turns back towards the Cortina.

Cut to Cortina. Gwenda opens the driver's door and gets in.

MRS TRELLIS (*out of view*). . . . And the next thing I know, she's going on about the sherry glasses . . . !

The door closes and silences her. The Constable comes into frame and bends to speak to Gwenda just as the engine starts, and the Cortina accelerates violently away. The Constable straightens up and watches it go in surprise.

Cut to:

64. Interior. 1100/Exterior. Dual carriageway. Day.

Laura driving, Stimpson beside her, gazing unseeing at the road ahead.

STIMPSON (*voice over*). An attack upon the whole social order . . .

His eyes flick down to the watch on his wrist.

Cut to close up of watch. It shows 12.36.

Cut to Stimpson. He gazes unseeing at the road ahead again.

STIMPSON (*voice over*). More than that, it is an offence against nature itself. (*To Laura.*) Ten o'clock in the morning?

LAURA. What?

STIMPSON. You had a row with your boy-friend at ten o'clock in the morning?

LAURA. I had a free.

STIMPSON. Study periods are for study, Laura. The evening is the proper time to have rows with your boy-friend. (*Voice over.*) Does the tide ever come in behind the hour appointed for it in the tide-tables?

LAURA. I couldn't see him in the evening.

STIMPSON (*voice over*). Does the sun ever appear late above the horizon, saying, Please, sir, the bus was full, the train was on strike?

LAURA. His wife wouldn't let him go out in the evening.

STIMPSON (*voice over*). If the sun depended on public transport to arrive each day, then you may be sure it would get up a little earlier. (*To Laura.*) His wife?

LAURA. It's OK. He didn't get on with her.

STIMPSON (*digests this. Sarcastically*). I suppose you *have* passed the driving test, Laura?

LAURA. As good as.

STIMPSON. What's that supposed to mean?

LAURA. I only failed on one thing.

STIMPSON (*decisively*). Right! Pull in! Now, please! At once!

Cut to Exterior. 1100. Pan with it as it pulls over on to the shoulder of the road and stops. Stimpson gets out of the nearside door and walks firmly round to the driver's door.

Cut to driver's door. Stimpson opens it, and waits while Laura reluctantly begins to get out.

STIMPSON. Let's get one thing straight, at any rate.

Cut to Police patrol car. Pan with it as it passes the 1100, then pulls over and stops on the shoulder a hundred yards in front.

Cut to Interior. Police patrol car. The two Policemen inside, seen from behind. They have turned round to look through their rear window.

FIRST POLICEMAN (*dubiously*). Blue 1100 . . .

SECOND POLICEMAN. Million blue 1100s.

FIRST POLICEMAN. Middle-aged man and a girl . . .

The Second Policeman makes a marginal face.

Cut to Exterior. Police patrol car. It begins to reverse.

Cut to Interior. 1100. Laura, in the passenger's seat, is looking at Stimpson, nettled. Stimpson is looking down at the unfamiliar controls. His good humour has been restored by his decisiveness.

STIMPSON. That's life, I'm afraid, Laura. *You* can drive, but you haven't passed the test.

He looks over his shoulder to see if it is clear for him to turn out, and lets the clutch in.

STIMPSON. *I*, on the other hand, *have* passed the test, but . . .

A crash. They are both flung forward.

Cut to Exterior. The two cars.

The 1100, as it moved forward, has crashed into the back of the reversing police patrol car.

Cut to close up of an item of trim, as it falls off the 1100 and into the road. Then silence.

Cut to close up of Stimpson. He sits absolutely still, and closes his eyes.

Cut to close up of Laura. She has her hands pressed to her mouth in shock and disbelief. She turns to look at Stimpson.

Cut to close up of Stimpson. He opens his eyes, and gives a very small sigh.

Cut to Exterior. The two cars.

The doors of the police patrol car open, and the two Policemen get out. They walk back without hurry to view the damage.

Cut to Exterior 1100. Stimpson gets out, and comes

forward to meet the Policemen. He is appalled, but he sneaks one quick look at his watch.

Cut to Exterior. Mr Jolly's van. Pan with it as it comes along the same main road.

Cut to Interior. Van. Close up of Mr Jolly at the wheel, hunched up with anxiety. He notices something at the side of the road ahead. He frowns and begins to slow down. There is the sound of a hooter, and he looks into his mirror.

Cut to Mr Jolly's point of view of mirror. Through the windscreen can be seen the 1100 and the police car at the side of the road. In the mirror is the reflection of Mr and Mrs Wisely on their motor-cycle behind.

Cut to Interior. Van. Close up of Mr Jolly. He abandons the attempt to stop, and accelerates away again. Whereupon there is a blast from a different hooter. He looks right.

Cut to Mr Jolly's point of view of Gwenda's Cortina. It is overtaking him. Mrs Way, in the passenger's seat in front, gives him a vaguely benevolent smile and wave.

Cut to Interior. Van. Close up of Mr Jolly. He swerves the wheel guiltily away, and puts a concealing hand up to the right hand side of his face.

Cut to Exterior. Roadside. Mr Jolly's van goes out of frame to reveal beyond it, as before, the Police patrol car and the 1100. Tighten on to their locked bumpers, as the patrol car is very gently edged away from the 1100.

Cut to close up of Second Policeman. He is standing watching this process sombrely, and putting his notebook away. He glances up towards Stimpson.

Cut to close up of Stimpson. He is standing watching the same process. He flinches just perceptibly at each twang of disentangling metal.

Cut to close up of Laura. She, too, stands sombrely watching the separation of the cars. She looks up sombrely at Stimpson.

Cut to Stimpson and Laura.

STIMPSON. Don't worry. We'll just pull the wing away from the wheel. We'll be all right.

*Cut to Exterior. 1100. Stimpson is heaving away at the
nearside wing, trying to bend it away from the wheel.
Laura is watching him sombrely.*

(*Between heaves.*) It'll all be covered, Laura . . . Your
Dad's insurance . . . *I'm* the one they'll summons . . . *I'm*
the one who'll have to tell your Dad . . .

Cut to the two Policemen, approaching from the patrol car.

FIRST POLICEMAN. Yes, and another thing. Have you stopped
for petrol anywhere?

*Cut to Stimpson, heaving at the wing. He gives a particularly
violent heave, as if in response to the question, and the whole
wing comes away in his hands.*

STIMPSON. Petrol?

*He looks from the Policeman to Laura, surprised, trying to
remember. Cut to the two Policemen. They look at Stimpson
with little liking or trust. Cut to close up of Laura. She waits
to see what Stimpson will do. Cut to Stimpson, holding the
detached wing.*

No — filled it up yesterday. Didn't we, Laura?

Cut to the two Policemen. They turn to look at Laura.

*Cut to close up of Laura. She nods, looking at the ground,
ashamed.*

*Cut to the two Policemen. They glance at each other, and
decide, rather reluctantly, to leave it at that. They go back
to the patrol car.*

*Cut to Stimpson and Laura. He looks at her, but she is
looking away. Pan with his as he goes to the driver's door.
He opens the door, then realises that he is still holding the
detached wing. He chucks it to the side of the road.*

Cut to Laura.

LAURA (*with great vehemence*). No! That's part of our car!

*Cut to Stimpson. He silently bows to this. Pan with him as
he crosses to recover the wing, then returns to the driver's
door. But when he gets there Laura is already occupying
the driver's seat. She looks at him defiantly. He gives in,
and walks round to the passenger's door on the nearside.*

Dissolve to:

65. Interior. 1100/Exterior. Road (1) to Norwich. Day.

Close up of Laura, driving, and Stimpson beside her.

LAURA. It's jangling all about. I can hear it. It's scratching the paint.

Cut to Exterior. 1100. The detached wing is on the roof rack, bouncing up and down with the car's motion.

Cut to Interior. 1100.

STIMPSON (*voice over*). At Thomas Tompion we insist upon certain traditional standards, we insist upon 12.58 . . . (*To Laura.*) We must find a phone. Warn them I'm not going to be there until four. (*Voice over.*) Does the tide ever go out during a Study Period, saying, Please, sir, I'm having a row with my boy-friend . . .? (*To Laura.*) It isn't someone on the staff, is it? It's not Mr Slidewell? Or Mr Fellowdew?

He turns to look at her. She shakes her head. Another rather more appallingly probable possibility comes to him.

It's not Mr Jolly?

LAURA. No.

Stimpson is not quite sure what this 'No' means. He turns to stare through the windscreen again, and draws in his breath in audible alarm.

I wasn't anywhere near him!

STIMPSON. You realise that if you're not licensed we're not insured? (*Voice over.*) 12.59.

Cut to:

66. Exterior. Telephone boxes. Day.

Pan with the 1100 as it pulls up at a row of three telephone boxes in a small town. Stimpson jumps out, holding a letter. Pan with him as he runs to the first telephone box. He stops at the door, pulls out his change and examines it, then turns back towards the 1100.

STIMPSON. 10p. Have you got 10p?

Cut to Laura in the 1100. She fishes a single 10p piece out of a pocket, and leans across the passenger's seat. Stimpson comes into shot, and takes the coin. Pan with him as he runs back to the first phone box. He pulls the door open, and comes face to face with a Man on Phone.

MAN ON PHONE (*into the receiver*). All right, then, in the

third race give me number four for a win, and number seven
for a place . . .

STIMPSON. Sorry.

*Pan with Stimpson as he moves on to the second phone
box and enter it. He picks up the receiver and puts it to
his ear. He jiggles the receiver rest up and down — takes the
receiver away from his ear and shakes it — rattles the
receiver rest violently up and down — then hurls the receiver
back on to the rest in disgust, and comes out of the box.*

*Pan with him to the third phone box. He goes in and picks
up the receiver. The dialling tone is just audible. He locates
the phone number on the letter he is holding, and dials it. He
misdials the third digit, shakes the receiver rest violently up
and down to restore the dialling tone, and starts to dial again.*

*Cut to the 1100. Laura, watching Stimpson rather sourly.
She looks quickly away.*

*Cut to Stimpson in third phone box. He is looking out in
Laura's direction, the receiver to his ear. The ringing tone
starts. He turns back to concentrate on the call, glancing
at his watch. He gets through.*

VOICE ON PHONE. University of East Anglia.

*The voice is immediately overlaid by peep-peep-peep.
Stimpson pushes his 10p into the slot. But it won't go.
He struggles wildly until he is cut off, and the dialling
tone returns. He slams the receiver down, comes out of the
box, then turns back and kicks savagely at it.*

*Cut to the 1100. Close up of Laura, watching Stimpson
expressionlessly.*

*Cut to Stimpson, outside third phone box. He makes
large gestures to demonstrate his frustration to Laura, then
goes back inside the box.*

Cut to:

67. Exterior/Interior. Pat's house — kitchen. Day.

*Exterior. Window of nearby house. An elderly woman,
Mrs Garden, twitches the net curtains aside and looks out,
narrowing her eyes.*

Cut to:

68. Interior/Exterior. Pat's house — kitchen. Day.

Interior. Mrs Garden's kitchen. Over the shoulder shot of Mrs Garden looking out at the row of telephone boxes. She is holding a steaming saucepan.

MRS GARDEN. They're vandalising those phones again, Pat.

   Cut to:

69. Interior. Pat's house — dining room. Day.

Interior. Mrs Garden's dining room. Pat Garden is just finishing laying an informal lunch for five. She is a jolly, joshing woman in middle age, though at the moment rather harassed. A bored, ten-year-old Child is sprawled on the floor at her feet, hindering her.

PAT (*calls*). All right, Mum. Just going.

CHILD. When's lunch?

PAT. Now! Granny's just bringing it!

MRS GARDEN (*out of view*). The phones, Pat! They're at the phones again!

PAT (*calls*). Just put my woolly on! (*To Child.*) Tell Tom and Boo lunch is on the table.

   Cut to:

70. Exterior. Telephone boxes. Day.

Interior. Third phone box. Stimpson has the receiver to his ear. He gets through.

VOICE ON PHONE. University of East Anglia.

   Peep-peep-peep, as before. As before, Stimpson tries to put his 10p in the slot, and, as before, it won't go. He gives a great roar of exasperation and slams the receiver down. He barges out of the box, glaring in the direction of the car.

   Cut to the 1100. Close up of Laura. She indicates the first phone box.

   Cut to Stimpson outside the third phone box. He turns to look at the first phone box.

   Cut to first phone box. The Man on Phone who was occupying it before is just coming out.

*Cut to Stimpson, outside the third phone box. He waves
thank-you to Laura. Pan with him as he goes to the first
phone box.*

Cut to:

71. Interior. Pat's house — kitchen. Day.

*Interior. Mrs Garden's kitchen. Mrs Garden at the window. She
has put the saucepan down, and is now holding a telephone
receiver to her ear.*

MRS GARDEN (*calls*). Girl and a boy. He's showing off his
muscles, she's egging him on. (*Into phone.*) Hello, is that
the police . . . ?

Cut to:

72. Interior. Pat's house — hall. Day.

Pat is just pulling on a cardigan.

PAT (*calls*). I'll try and keep them talking till the police
get here.

She opens the front door.

Cut to:

73. Exterior. Telephone boxes. Day.

Stimpson has the receiver to his ear. He gets through.

VOICE ON PHONE. University of East Anglia.

*Peep-peep-peep, as before. Stimpson pushes the 10p into
the slot, and it goes effortlessly. The peeping ceases.*

University of East Anglia.

STIMPSON. Thank God. Look, I'm calling long distance and
I've only got one 10p, so could you please take a message
and pass it on to the Secretary of the Headmasters'
Conference?

VOICE ON PHONE. University of East Anglia?

STIMPSON. Yes, our Annual Meeting is being held there. It
starts at five o'clock. Would you tell him I was supposed to
be there at three . . .

VOICE ON PHONE. Hello? University of East Anglia.

STIMPSON. Can't you hear me? I said, would you tell him
    I'm going to be slightly . . .

VOICE ON PHONE. Put your money into the box, caller.

STIMPSON (*screaming*). I've *put* my money into the box!
    It's eaten the money! I haven't *got* any more money!

*Dialling tone. Stimpson goes beserk. He kicks the coin
box, and hammers the receiver on it.*

*Cut to Pat, standing outside the phone box, sombrely
watching the performance inside. She turns to look
reproachfully at Laura.*

*Cut to Laura, in the 1100. Laura turns and looks away,
embarrassed at knowing Stimpson.*

*Cut to Stimpson, in the first coin box. He hammers the
receiver down on the coin-box again, and the earpiece
springs off. He gazes at the truncated receiver. Sobriety
rapidly returns. He puts the remains of the receiver down
and leaves. He comes face to face with Pat.*

PAT (*insultingly*). How old are you?

STIMPSON (*embarrassed*). It's out of order.

PAT (*in a different voice*). I'll tell you how old you are.
    You're two years and one day older than me.

STIMPSON. I mean, it took the money, and . . . Pat!

PAT. Well, fancy meeting you like this!

STIMPSON. Good God!

PAT. You don't *live* here?

STIMPSON. No, no. I'm . . . (*Glances at his watch.*)

PAT. I don't live here! I don't even live in England! I'm just
    seeing my Mum!

STIMPSON. Isn't that amazing! Well . . .

PAT. Anyway, Brian, you don't have to tell me what *you're*
    up to these days, because I can see. You're late!

STIMPSON (*glancing at his watch*). No, no. It was the third
    phone in a row . . .

PAT. Still late for everything, are you, Brian?

STIMPSON. I'm *not* late these days, as a matter of fact. But it took the money . . .

PAT. What was it this time, Brian? Buses on strike? Got on the wrong train?

STIMPSON. I'm not late!

PAT. I'd say come and have lunch . . .

STIMPSON (*looks at his watch*). Unfortunately . . .

PAT. All right, Brian. Just your luck, isn't it, running into someone you haven't seen for twenty years when you're late already?

STIMPSON (*reasonably*). I'm not late — I'm merely in a hurry.

PAT. Give me a kiss, then, and I'll let you run.

She kisses him firmly on the lips, and embraces him warmly. He has to respond by putting his arms round her. He glances in the direction of the 1100 over her shoulder.

PAT. Been lovely to see you, Brian . . .

Cut to Laura, in the 1100. She is watching with interest, but now looks quickly away.

Cut to:

74. Exterior/Interior. Pat's house — kitchen. Day.

Exterior. Mrs Garden's kitchen window. The net curtain is twitched aside again, and Mrs Garden peers out in amazement at the development of the scene.

Cut to:

75. Exterior. Telephone boxes. Day.

Pat and Stimpson, embracing. He looks at his watch over her shoulder. Pat breaks free.

PAT. Here, come on. I'll give you Mum's number. You can phone me when you've got a moment.

She leads him over to the 1100, and bends down to talk to Laura through the open driver's window, getting a pencil and paper out of her pocket as she does so.

PAT. You won't believe this, but your Dad and I were at

Training College together! And he was late for everything!
He was late the first time he took me out; he was late
every time he took me out; he was late the day he collected
his diploma!

Laura giggles nervously.

Oh, he hasn't told you about all that!

She turns in humorous reproach to Stimpson.

Haven't you told her about your murky past, then?

But Stimpson isn't listening. He is gazing down the road.

*Cut to Stimpson's point of view of Police panda car
approaching and pulling up behind the 1100.*

PAT (*out of view*). He's not even listening.

*Cut to Stimpson and Pat. Stimpson is still intent upon the
panda car.*

PAT (*to Stimpson*). I said you're not even listening!

STIMPSON (*vaguely*). I suppose not.

He bends down, and speaks sharply but privately to Laura.

Out!

Laura looks round, and sees the panda car.

*Cut to Police panda car. The Policeman gets out, and stands
feeling in his hip pocket for a notebook, gazing absently as
he does so at the 1100.*

Cut to Exterior. 1100.

Laura gets smartly out of the car.

PAT (*gives Stimpson the number she has written down*). Well,
I can see your mind's on other things. I mustn't hold you
up . . .

STIMPSON. Yes, we must be on our way.

He opens the driver's door to get in.

LAURA. No!

She slams the door shut again.

PAT (*amused*). Oh, she won't let poor old Dad drive, will she?

LAURA (*embarrassed but obstinate*). No, I won't.

PAT (*seriously*). She's lovely, Brian. Real glint in her eye.

STIMPSON (*preoccupied with the police again*). Yes . . . Pat, can you drive?

PAT. Great to see you again, anyway . . . Can I drive?

STIMPSON. You've passed your test? You've got a licence?

PAT. Yes . . . What's all this about?

Stimpson opens the driver's door of the 1100.

STIMPSON. Have a drive. Go on — see what you think of it. (*To Laura.*) All right? (*To Pat.*) Just round the block!

In the back of the shot the Policeman can be seen walking towards the telephone boxes. Pat hesitates, glancing at the car. It doesn't look the sort of car that proud owners invite you to try out.

STIMPSON. I'd like to know what you think! Go on!

PAT. I thought you were late?

STIMPSON. I'm not late!

PAT. Funny man you are, Brian.

Pat gets dubiously into the driver's seat. Laura goes reluctantly round and gets into the front passenger seat. Stimpson quickly slams the door and gets into the back.

Cut to Interior. 1100.

Pat gamely but uncomprehendingly works out where all the controls are. Stimpson, in the back, follows the movements of the Policeman.

PAT. Haven't driven in this country for twenty years.

STIMPSON. Never mind. Off we go.

PAT. Married to a dentist Down Under.

STIMPSON. Really? Come on, then.

Cut to Stimpson's point of view of Policeman. He comes out of the first phone box, holding the mutilated receiver. He looks up and down the road.

PAT (*out of view*). I've brought the kids over to stay with Mum. We're just going to have lunch!

STIMPSON (*out of view*). Right. Let's go.

Cut to Interior. 1100.

PAT (*to Laura*). You've got time for lunch, haven't you? I bet you're starving! I've got one your age!

LAURA. Well, I am rather . . .

STIMPSON. Later, later! Get this drive over first!

Cut to Stimpson's point of view of Policeman. He puts the receiver back in the box, and strolls over towards the 1100.

PAT. All right. Once round the block, then. Close your eyes and pray!

Cut to Interior. 1100.

PAT. On the left still, isn't it?

STIMPSON (*abstracted*). Right.

The Policeman's head comes into frame, lowered to the level of the open driver's window. He opens his mouth to speak. But Pat has turned to look at Stimpson.

PAT. On the *right*?

STIMPSON. Left! Left!

PAT. Right.

She turns to face front, and the car disappears from frame in a couple of great kangaroo leaps, leaving the Policeman with his mouth still open to speak.

Cut to Mrs Garden, approaching from the direction of her house as fast as she can.

MRS GARDEN. Stop them! Stop them!

Cut to Policeman.

POLICEMAN. What, them? They did the phone?

Cut to Mrs Garden.

MRS GARDEN. The phone, yes! And now they've kidnapped my daughter.

Cut to:

76. Interior. 1100/Exterior. Road near telephone boxes. Day.

Pat driving, Laura beside her, Stimpson visible between them in the back. He is looking anxiously out of the rear window.

PAT. Yes, well, it's fine. It's lovely.

STIMPSON (*turns back sharply*). What?

PAT. The car.

STIMPSON. Oh. Right.

He turns to look out of the rear window. There is a boingling noise from the loose wing on the roof.

PAT. There's perhaps something not quite right up here somewhere. (*Indicates roof.*)

LAURA (*tautly*). That's the wing.

PAT. The wing?

LAURA. He pulled it off. Dad'll kill me.

Pat looks uncertainly at Laura out of the corner of her eye, and at Stimpson in the mirror. Stimpson is still absorbed in the view out of the rear window, but Laura realises that a certain discrepancy has now come to light.

LAURA. It's Dad's car. It's not *his* car! *He's* not my father! He's Mr Stimpson! (*To Stimpson.*) Why did you tell her I was your daughter?

Cut to Stimpson. He is looking out of the rear window. He becomes aware that something has been said, and turns back to the front.

STIMPSON. Daughter? Who, me? No, son. I haven't got a daughter.

Cut to Pat. She is giving Stimpson a very odd look in the mirror.

Cut to all three.

STIMPSON. What, Laura? Laura's one of my girls!

He gets another look from Pat in the mirror.

One of my sixth-formers! She's very kindly driving me to Norwich. It's the Headmasters' Conference. I'm a headmaster now!

PAT (*coldly*). Yes, well, I'll say goodbye, then, Brian.

She slows down to stop. Stimpson takes a hasty look out of the rear window. Faint sound of a police siren.

STIMPSON. You can't stop here.

PAT. It's all right, I'll walk back.

STIMPSON. Police-car . . .

PAT (*drives on*). It's your life, Brian. I don't want to say anything. I just don't want to get involved.

STIMPSON. Keep going! Keep going!

PAT. We'll be out in the country in a minute. My children don't know where I am. We're just sitting down to lunch!

STIMPSON. It's all right — we'll find a bus-stop.

PAT (*alarmed at the distance this implies*). Find a bus-stop?

LAURA. Here's a bus-stop.

STIMPSON. You can't stop on a bus-stop!

PAT (*panic growing*). Where am I going?

STIMPSON (*glances right*). Straight out!

　　Cut to:

77. Exterior. Junction at road near telephone boxes and main road. Day.

Exterior. Turn out on to main road. The 1100 comes straight out on to the main road, just squeezing in front of a large lorry, which brakes and blasts its horn and flashes its lights. The police panda car appears at the turnout, but is forced to stop by the lorry.

Cut to:

78. Interior. 1100/Exterior. Main road (2) to Norwich. Day.

Interior. 1100. The lorry can be seen through the rear window, threateningly close, and still blasting its horn.

STIMPSON. Well done.

PAT (*in a state*). Hooting . . .

STIMPSON. Don't mind him.

PAT. I don't know where we are! I don't know where we're going!

STIMPSON. I'll tell you. Hold on. (*Consults the road atlas.*)

PAT. It was always the same thing!

LAURA. You feel sorry for them, don't you?

PAT (*to Laura*). You'd start off in an evening dress and silver dance shoes, and you'd end up running, with your skirt in your hand, and your heel down a grating.

LAURA. Then they turn round and scream at you.

STIMPSON. Next left. Be posted to Northampton.

PAT (*screams*). Northampton?

STIMPSON. We'll put you on the train.

PAT. What do you mean, you'll put me on the train? They're sitting round the table! They're waiting to start lunch!

Faint sound of police siren. Stimpson glances out of the rear window.

STIMPSON. Get a move on, then. Put your foot down.

PAT. It's like being nineteen again! I hated being nineteen!

Cut to:

79. Exterior. Junction of main roads (3) to Norwich. Day.

Exterior. Main road. Track with the 1100 as it overtakes in the outside lane.

Cut to:

80. Interior. 1100/Exterior. Main road (3) to Norwich. Day.

Interior. 1100. Stimpson is gazing alternately out of the rear window and at the road atlas.

STIMPSON (*distractedly*). Right. Fine.

PAT (*terrified*). We shouldn't be doing this kind of speed! Not in a car like this!

STIMPSON. Right. Right.

PAT. Listen to it! It's coming to pieces!

The wing on the roof is indeed very active at this speed.

STIMPSON. Terrible. Terrible.

PAT. *Now* where am I going? I'm going left, am I?

STIMPSON (*distracted*). Right. Right.

PAT. Right?

   Cut to:

81. Exterior. Junction of main roads (3) and (4) to Norwich. Day.

Exterior. Left turn from main road. The 1100 is starting to make the left turn, then suddenly, at the last moment, changes direction. It crosses the white hatching on the road and carries straight on. Various other vehicles turn left. The police panda car follows them left, then at the last moment attempts to change direction to go straight on. But the lorry is coming up fast in the inside lane. There is a blast of horn, and the police panda car is forced to swerve back on to its original track and turn left.

Cut to:

82. Interior. 1100/Exterior. Road (4) to Norwich. Day.

Interior. 1100. Stimpson is looking out of the rear window.

STIMPSON. All right. Ten minutes, and we'll be in Northampton.

LAURA. Northampton was left.

STIMPSON (*incredulous*). That was our turn?

PAT. You said right!

STIMPSON (*in his child-shattering voice*). I said *left*!

PAT. Look, Brian, don't you shout at me!

STIMPSON. Can't *anyone* tell left from right?

LAURA. She's doing her best!

STIMPSON (*rigidly polite again*). Right. Just take the next left, will you?

PAT. I'll get straight out of the car!

STIMPSON. You can't get out of the car now until we get to Northampton.

PAT. Always late. Always trying to make it my fault. Always screaming at me.

STIMPSON (*patiently*). I wasn't screaming. I was merely saying . . . left. Left.

PAT. And now they've made you a headmaster? It's like putting a shark in charge of a swimming-pool!

STIMPSON (*patiently*). Left . . . Left . . . (*his patience breaks*). LEFT! LEFT! LEFT!

Cut to:

83. Exterior. Side road off road (4) to Norwich. Day.

Exterior. Small side road turning off from the main road. Pan with 1100 as it makes a belated 90 degree left turn.

Cut to:

84. Interior. 1100/Exterior. Side Road. Day.

Laura picks herself out of Pat's lap. Stimpson detaches himself from the right hand side of the car.

PAT (*panicky*). What's this? This isn't going anywhere!

STIMPSON (*with iron calm*). It's going back to the Northampton Road.

PAT. They'll be out of their minds!

STIMPSON. Just keep absolutely calm, and turn left, and left again. So left here . . .

She turns blindly.

PAT. I don't know what I'm doing.

STIMPSON. Perfect. Thank you. Well done. Now, we just go round the next corner, and . . .

They are all hurled forward as Pat brakes.

Cut to:

85. Exterior. Road with cows. Day.

Exterior. 1100. It has just turned a corner in a very narrow lane, and come face to face with a herd of cows.

Cut to Interior. 1100.

PAT (*tensely*). Now what?

STIMPSON (*very patient*). Don't worry. We just go back.

PAT. Back?

STIMPSON. Right. Reverse.

PAT. How did this happen to me?

STIMPSON (*with absolute patience*). In reverse gear . . . Put it into reverse.

PAT. Reverse?

STIMPSON. Show her where reverse is, Laura.

Laura mutely puts the gear into reverse. Pat turns round and lets the clutch in. Stimpson turns to look out of the rear window.

STIMPSON. Good. Well done. Come on. Come on, come on . . . *Stop!*

Cut to Exterior. 1100. It has stopped a few feet away from a lorry loaded with milk churns that has appeared round the corner behind the car and also stopped, blocking the lane completely.

Cut to Interior. 1100. Close up of Pat, still turned to look out of the rear window for reversing. She closes her eyes.

Cut to close up of Stimpson. He turns from the rear window to face forwards. He, too, has his eyes closed.

STIMPSON (*voice over*). This is a historic moment. Little did I dream that I should be sitting here . . .

Cut to close up of cow. It gazes in through the window of the car, ruminating quietly.

Cut to close up of Laura. She looks at the cow.

LAURA. When are we going to have lunch?

Cut to close up of Pat. She opens her eyes wearily.

Cut to close up of Stimpson. He opens his eyes wearily.

STIMPSON (*in quiet command*). Into the field.

PAT (*quietly*). Into the field?

STIMPSON (*quietly but firmly*). Just do as I say.

Pat turns to face front and quietly obeys.

Cut to Exterior. 1100. It escapes out of the lane through the open gateway beside it.

Cut to:

86. Exterior. Track in field. Day.

Pan with the 1100 as it comes through the gateway into the field, and bounces up a rough track.

Cut to:

87. Interior. 1100/Exterior. Track in field. Day.

Interior. 1100. All three occupants are bouncing wildly up and down.

STIMPSON (*looking at road atlas*). We'll get something to eat in Northampton. We're going to hit the road in about a hundred yards.

PAT (*tears in her eyes*). I know this is wrong! I know it! I know it!

STIMPSON (*calmly and firmly*). It'll be just beyond that hedge.

   Cut to:

88. Exterior. Fields. Day.

Exterior. Field. Pan with a tractor, ploughing. The Driver of the tractor is a solid, slow man. His attention is caught by the 1100 which appears behind him, a long way off, gradually overtaking him on a parallel course along the track. It follows the track to a gap in the hedge, and disappears.

Cut to Exterior. Next field, where the track emerges from a gap in the hedge. The 1000 comes through the gap and stops.

Cut to Interior. 1100. All three occupants gaze sombrely forward at the view.

Cut to over the shoulder shot through windscreen. An open green meadow stretches downhill in front of the car. The next hedge is a long way away, and there is a broad view beyond it.

STIMPSON. Just beyond the *next* hedge.

   Cut to all three occupants of the car from in front. Laura turns to glance at Pat. Pat's face says that the road is not just beyond the next hedge.

STIMPSON. Look, I can see the cars! I can see them moving!

   Pat and Laura's faces say that they cannot.

Right, then.

LAURA. There's no track. We've come to the end of the track.

STIMPSON. We don't need a track. It's grass. Come on.

Pat gives a sob. She lets the clutch in.

Cut to Exterior. First field. The Tractor Driver takes his machine up to the hedge that divides the field from the meadow, and stops. He gazes over the hedge from the vantage-point offered by the tractor. In the meadow beyond, the 1100 can be seen jouncing slowly forward over the open grass.

Cut to close up of the Tractor Driver. He switches off the engine to the tractor, and settles down to watch.

Cut to:

89. Exterior. Fields (aerial shot). Day.

Tracking shot of 1100 from helicopter. Track close with it as it bounces its way across the meadow, then gradually pull out and up to reveal that there is no road beyond the next hedge. Keep widening to reveal the whole breadth of the country in front of the car.

STIMPSON (*voice over*). Perhaps I sound a little old-fashioned. But, you know, we live in a world where time is becoming not less important, but ever more so. Imagine a spacecraft running late! It might miss its orbit completely, and find itself wandering off into the trackless depths of the universe!

Cut to:

90. Exterior. Sky. Day.

A hawk, hovering and soaring. Music over. Suddenly the hawk swoops. The music fades into the sound of a car engine revving wildly.

Cut to:

91. Exterior. Fields. Day.

The 1100 is stuck in the mud. Its engine is screaming.

Cut to close up of wingless nearside front wheel. It is spinning wildly, hurling a great spray of mud back.

Cut to Interior 1100. The engine is still screaming.

PAT (*shaking her head, dazed*). Nightmare. Nightmare.

STIMPSON (*very calm and reasonable*). Hold it, Pat. Hold it. Let's just have a quiet think.

PAT (*unheeding*). Never going to get home.

The engine note rises and rises. Pat evidently has her foot flat on the floor. Stimpson waits patiently.

LAURA (*suddenly*). Stop it! You'll break the engine!

Pat takes her foot off the accelerator. She closes her eyes.

STIMPSON (*to Pat*). Thank you. Thank you, Laura. Now, it's five to two.

LAURA. I'm hungry.

STIMPSON (*reasonably*). You're hungry. We're all hungry. But we can't eat now, because we're in the middle of a field. So — we have to adapt to our circumstances.

He gets out of the car.

Cut to Exterior 1100. Stimpson stands by the car, and addresses Pat and Laura inside it.

I wanted to be in Norwich at three, to greet everyone as they arrived. I can't be there at three. So instead I want to be there at five, in time to deliver my speech. This is how mankind has evolved from the primeval slime — by adapting to circumstances. We can't go forwards. So we'll go backwards instead. Put it in reverse for her, Laura. I'll push.

He walks round to the front of the car, and leans against the bonnet just above the wingless near wheel.

Right? Right!

He sets his shoulder to the radiator and his ear to the bonnet and pushes with all his strength. The engine note rises as before.

Cut to close up of Pat, gripping the steering wheel, and willing the car to move. In her face is written all the effort being expended externally by Stimpson. Pan to Laura. In her face is written all the agony of the tortured engine.

Cut to close up of wingless nearside front wheel. Spinning in reverse, it is now throwing up a spray of mud forward. Loosen steadily to show where it is going — over the straining torso of Stimpson. Suddenly he gives up and springs upright. He is covered from neck to feet in mud.

Cut to Interior. 1100. Pat and Laura. They gaze at the transformed Stimpson. The engine note dies away, awestruck.

Cut to Stimpson. He presses his hands to his face, then takes them away, leaving his face now in much the same state as his suit. Then suddenly his rage bursts forth. He kicks wildly out at the car, as at the telephone box earlier. But the kick makes him lose his footing in the mud, and he falls down. He scrambles to his feet, then stands for an instant in raging indecision.

Cut to Pat and Laura, still staring at Stimpson. Laura glances at Pat, then back at Stimpson, and opens her mouth to speak.

Cut to Stimpson. He raises a hand to silence her.

STIMPSON. No! Thank you! Wait there! Don't move!

He runs off.

Cut to Pat and Laura, in the 1100. Laura turns to look at Pat again.

PAT (*in a state of shock*). Why me, though? Why me?

Cut to Tractor Driver, as before, sitting on his tractor, peaceably eating a sandwich, and observing the scene in the meadow beyond the hedge.

STIMPSON (*calls out of view*). Excuse me . . . Hello . . . !

Cut to over the shoulder shot. The Tractor Driver in the foreground, looking over the hedge at the meadow. Away down at the bottom of the meadow is the 1100. Struggling uphill towards the Tractor Driver as fast as he can is the mud-covered, breathless Stimpson.

Can you tell me . . . ? Do you know . . . ? Is there anyone round here with a tractor?

Cut to reverse. Over the shoulder shot with Stimpson in the foreground. The top part of the Tractor Driver can be seen over the hedge. The tractor itself is invisible.

TRACTOR DRIVER (*unhurriedly*). Won my bet, anyway. Watched you go down the meadow there. Bet myself a cheese sandwich you wouldn't get as far as the bottom.

He holds up the sandwich, and takes another bite.

Cut to reverse, favouring Stimpson.

STIMPSON (*demonstrating ruefulness*). Right. We're stuck. We need a tractor to pull us out.

TRACTOR DRIVER. Having a day in the country, are you?

STIMPSON. Not really. Is there a farm near here?

TRACTOR DRIVER. Getting close to nature?

He nods at Stimpson's suit. Stimpson glances down.

STIMPSON (*forces a laugh*). Right! Right! We're in rather a hurry, you see. I've got to be in Norwich by five.

TRACTOR DRIVER. Norwich? You're going to Norwich?

STIMPSON. Yes, so if we can just find a tractor . . .

TRACTOR DRIVER. What, short cut, is it?

STIMPSON. Lost our way. So we must quickly find a tractor.

TRACTOR DRIVER. Well, my advice is this.

STIMPSON. Yes?

TRACTOR DRIVER. If you're going this way . . .

STIMPSON. Yes?

TRACTOR DRIVER. Find a tractor . . .

Cut to Stimpson.

STIMPSON (*impatiently*). A tractor — yes.

Cut to Tractor Driver.

TRACTOR DRIVER. And stay on the bloody thing all the way to Norwich.

Cut to Stimpson.

STIMPSON. Thank you. Thank you very much.

He writes off the Tractor Driver and cuts his losses. Pan with him as he turns and hurries away.

TRACTOR DRIVER (*out of view*). I'll tell you another thing.

STIMPSON. Yes. Thank you.

He keeps hurrying away.

Cut to the Tractor Driver.

TRACTOR DRIVER (*calls*). Know what I'm sitting on?

Cut to Stimpson. Pan with him as he keeps hurrying away from the Tractor Driver.

STIMPSON (*to himself*). A bomb, I hope.

Cut to the Tractor Driver. Dusts the sandwich crumbs off his fingers.

TRACTOR DRIVER (*to himself*). All right, my old dear. You look that way — I'll look this. And I bet you a jam tart I find a tractor first.

He takes a jam tart out of his lunch box, and holds it between his teeth while he prepares to start his engine.

Cut to:

92. Exterior. Door in wall. Day.

Stimpson is pulling at an old-fashioned bell-rope. The sound of the bell can be heard, somewhere in the remoteness of the house beyond, together with a faint, distant sound of chanting.

STIMPSON (*to himself, impatiently*). Come on, come on.

A grille opens in the door, and a man's face looks out. Stimpson does not see it. He pulls at the bell-rope again.

Oh, for God's sake! Turn the record-player down!

He turns and hammers on the door with his fists, which brings him eye-to-eye with the face and the grille.

Ah! Right. There you are. Now. A tractor. I'm looking for a tractor. You don't have a tractor here, do you?

The grille closes. There is the sound of a key turning in a lock, and the door swings open. Stimpson enters.

I'm so sorry! But it is rather urgent. I have to be in Norwich by . . .

He turns, inside the gate, and looks back at the man who has opened it. His voice dies away.

Cut to reverse shot, with Stimpson in the foreground looking back at the man who has let him in. He is a Monk. He gestures gravely for Stimpson to accompany him.

(*To himself, bitterly.*) Of course. A Monastery. I might have guessed.

Cut to:

93. Exterior. Fields. Day.

Pan with the Tractor Driver as he drives up to the 1100.

TRACTOR DRIVER. Heading for Norwich, I believe.

PAT (*with restraint*). Some of us.

The Tractor Driver jumps down from the tractor and begins to attach a tow chain to the back of the car.

TRACTOR DRIVER. Dodged the traffic, anyway.

Cut to:

94. Interior. Refectory. Day.

A large, bare room inside the monastery, furnished with folding wooden tables and benches. Stimpson is sitting on one of these benches, alone in the room. He is still covered in mud.

Pause. Then he becomes aware of the slow, uneven ticking of a clock. He looks round. There is no clock to be seen — only bare white walls. He waits in patience. The sound of a door opening. He turns to look.

Cut to door of the room. The Prior has come in. He is a silent, shy, withdrawn man. Pan with him as he crosses to a bench some way away from Stimpson and sits down, gazing at him.

Cut to Stimpson.

STIMPSON. Have they found a tractor?

Cut to Prior. He shakes his head gravely, and continues to look at Stimpson.

Cut to Stimpson.

Well . . . It doesn't matter. It wasn't important . . .

Cut to Prior. He gazes at Stimpson. Time goes by.

Cut to Stimpson.

I'm sorry to let them down, that's all . . . It doesn't matter to *me* . . . It was important for the school — it would have meant so much to the children . . . Well . . .

He shrugs, and writes the trip off. Pause. The clock ticks.

I suppose we couldn't ring for a taxi?

Cut to Prior. He shakes his head.

Cut to Stimpson.

No phone?

Cut to Prior. He makes a slight gesture of polite regret.

It would have meant a lot to my mother, of course . . . If she'd been alive . . . I mean, *I'd* be happy to enter a monastery and never speak again.

PRIOR (*after a pause*). We speak.

Cut to Stimpson.

STIMPSON. I'm sorry. I just assumed . . . I'm sorry . . .

Pause. The clock ticks. Stimpson thinks. He runs a hand through his hair, then passes it over his face. It leaves a trail of mud.

STIMPSON. What do you think I should do, then?

Cut to Prior. He thinks.

PRIOR. Have a bath, perhaps?

Cut to:

95. Exterior. Backyard of monastery. Day.

A Monk cycles through the gates, leading a short procession which consists of the tractor, driven by the Tractor Driver, towing the 1100 backwards, with Pat and Laura still sitting in it. The procession comes to a halt.

Cut to Tractor Driver.

TRACTOR DRIVER. Funny old boy-friend you girls have found yourselves.

He jumps down and walks back to the 1100.

Takes you out for a bit of nature study in the country, then slips off and enters a monastery.

He goes to the back of the car to take off the tow-chain.

Pat. Right. I'm off.

LAURA (*to Pat*). Mr Stimpson . . .

PAT. Are you coming with me or aren't you?

LAURA (*gets out*). It's our car!

PAT. I'm not waiting.

LAURA (*calls desperately*). Mr Stimpson!

  Cut to:

96. Interior. Corridor. Day.

Track with a Monk who is carrying a spare pair of sandals and a spare habit. He holds the habit up as he walks, checking it, then places it outside a closed door in the corridor. There is a sound of bathwater splashing. The Monk picks up the muddy suit and shoes lying outside the door, then stops before he takes them away, listening to another sound that is now coming through the door. It is Stimpson singing.

STIMPSON (*out of view*). He who would valiant be
                    'Gainst all disaster
                    Let him in constancy
                    Follow the Master.

  The Monk creeps respectfully away with the suit and shoes.

  Cut to:

97. Interior. Bathroom. Day.

A bare room with an old-fashioned bath and an ancient geyser above it. Stimpson is lying in the bath, completely at peace, singing abstractedly to himself.

STIMPSON.   There's no discouragement
                    Shall make him once relent
                    His first avowed intent
                    To be . . .

LAURA (*calls, out of view*). Mr Stimpson!

  Stimpson stops singing and listens. He has not quite heard. He starts the next verse.

STIMPSON.   Whoso beset him round
                    With dismal stories
                    Do but themselves . . .

LAURA (*out of view*). Mr Stimpson!

  This time Stimpson has heard. He sits up in the bath, all his composure gone.

  Cut to:

98. Exterior. Monastery garden. Day.

Laura is looking round hopelessly.

LAURA. Quick! Where are you?

A first floor window is flung up, and Stimpson looks out, with no clothes on and water running off him.

LAURA. It's your friend! She won't wait!

STIMPSON. They can't find a tractor!

LAURA. We've got one! It's pulled us out . . . ! What are you doing?

STIMPSON. I'm having a bath . . . You've got one?

LAURA. She's going.

STIMPSON. I'll be right down.

The window is abruptly closed. Laura becomes aware that she is being stared at.

Cut to:

99. Exterior. Ground floor window. Day.

Several monks are gazing out at Laura with solemn interest.

Cut to:

100. Exterior. Monastery garden. Day.

Laura. Confused, she runs off.

Cut to:

101. Exterior. Ground floor window. Day.

Monks at the window. They turn to watch her go.

Cut to:

102. Exterior. Backyard. Day.

Pat is sitting at the wheel with the engine running, jabbing impatiently at the accelerator. Laura runs up.

PAT. Well?

LAURA. He's having a bath!

PAT. A bath? Why not a sauna and massage as well?

She drives off at speed.

Cut to:

103. Exterior. Back door. Day.

Stimpson comes running out, in his underwear, with sandals on his feet, his head concealed inside the monk's habit that he is still trying to drag on. As he comes out, so Laura goes running in, failing to recognise him.

LAURA (*calls*). Mr Stimpson!

STIMPSON (*stops, head still in habit*). Where is she?

Laura stops at the sound of the voice and returns.

LAURA. She's gone! I said, 'He's having a bath', and she went!

She points. Stimpson's head emerges from the habit, and turns to follow her finger.

Cut to:

104. Exterior. Lane by monastery. Day.

Point of view of the 1100. It is just slowing at the end of the drive before it turns out into the road.

Cut to:

105. Exterior. Back door. Day.

Laura and Stimpson.

STIMPSON. Stop her!

LAURA. It's our car!

They run down the drive after it.

Cut to:

106. Exterior. Window. Day.

The Prior is gazing gravely out in the direction of the drive.

Cut to:

107. Exterior. Another window. Day.

Several monks are looking out. One of them, a young man, is laughing and making excited gestures of encouragement. The others turn and look at him. He subsides.

Cut to:

108. Exterior. Lane outside monastery. Day.

Pan with Laura as she comes running out of the monastery gate, scarcely pausing as she looks up and down the lane.

LAURA. End of the lane!

> *She runs along the lane in pursuit. Pan with her as she passes a respectable-looking Woman of Low Church appearance who happens to be passing. Stop on the Woman as she turns to gaze after the fleeing Laura. She turns back to see Stimpson running past, in pursuit of Laura, wearing his monkish habit, his sandals going flop flop flop along the road. She purses her lips in disapproval.*
>
> *Cut to:*

109. Exterior. Junction of lane with main road (5). Day.

Laura runs out of the lane and stops, breathless, looking up and down the main road. Stimpson comes hobbling up to join her.

STIMPSON. Can't . . . sandals . . .

LAURA. We've found the road, anyway.

STIMPSON. It's not the despair, Laura. I can stand the despair. It's the hope.

LAURA (*points*). There!

> *She starts to run along the main road. Stimpson groans, and hobbles after her reluctantly.*
>
> *Cut to:*

110. Exterior. Roadside main road (5). Day.

The 1100, parked beside the main road, empty.

POLICEMAN (*out of view*). Blue Austin 1100, registration number GHJ 541 P.

> *Pan to the police patrol car parked in front of the 1100. One of the two Policemen is speaking into the microphone*

*of the police car's radio, the other is looking at the 1100
and writing in his notebook. Pat is standing by him, stony-
faced, waiting.*

POLICEMAN. We've also got Mrs Garden, reported missing
believed kidnapped. State of shock, otherwise appears all
right. No sign of the girl.

PAT (*expressionlessly*). She's at the monastery.

POLICEMAN (*into microphone*). Oh, she's apparently in a
monastery. No sign of the male suspect.

PAT. He's in the bath.

POLICEMAN (*into microphone*). He's in the bath. (*To Pat.*)
In the monastery? (*Into microphone.*) In the bath, in a
monastery. Going to take a bit of sorting out, this one.
We'll bring Mrs Garden in, anyway. We're charging her
with taking away and driving, driving a vehicle in an
unroadworthy condition, exceeding the speed limit, and
assaulting a police officer.

Cut to Exterior. Roadside.

*A quarter of a mile away. Laura, scarcely able to run
further. She stops and looks back at Stimpson, who is
hobbling well in the rear.*

LAURA (*calls to Stimpson*). Nearly there!

*She waits for him to catch up, and turns to look in the
direction of the 1100 again. Pan to 1100. The Policemen
are seeing Pat into the police car. Then one of them gets
into the driver's seat of the police car, and the other walks
back to the driver's door of the 1100.*

Cut to pan with Stimpson, as he hobbles towards Laura.

STIMPSON. One little slip, Laura . . . ! That's all . . . ! Said
right — meant left . . . One word . . . !

LAURA (*points, in dismay*). Going!

*Cut to point of view of the police car and 1100. They are
just pulling on to the road ahead and driving off.*

Cut to Exterior. Roadside.

*Laura and Stimpson. They are gazing after the departing
1100.*

Gone.

Pan with Stimpson as he totters across to a road sign and sinks down at the base of it. He pulls off his sandals and throws them away, one by one. His head sinks into his hands. He is finally defeated.

Cut to Laura. She sits down on the ground some little way off, glancing at Stimpson.

Cut to Stimpson. He eventually takes his head out of his hands.

STIMPSON. I've lied for this, Laura! I've stolen! I've taken you out of school! Well, I suppose this is a form of education. It's an education for *me*, Laura!

Cut to Laura. She is looking at Stimpson for the first time with sympathetic curiosity.

Cut to Stimpson. He looks at Laura.

You still haven't had any lunch.

Cut to Laura. She shakes her head slightly, still looking at him with interest.

Cut to Stimpson.

We'll get something . . .

He feels automatically for his wallet, and then realises what he is wearing.

Cut to Laura.

LAURA (*gravely*). In your suit?

Cut to Stimpson. He nods. He glances automatically at the watch on his wrist. But there is no watch on his wrist.

Cut to Laura.

In the bathroom?

Cut to Stimpson. He nods.

STIMPSON (*utterly dejected*). Even lost the time.

Cut to Laura. Pan with her as she gets up and comes over to sit by Stimpson. She puts a tentatively comforting hand on his arm.

Cut to:

111. Interior. Common room. University of East Anglia. Day.

Close up of digital clock on a wall. It shows 15.33. Pan down to First Headmaster. He is looking anxiously up at the clock. He checks it automatically against his watch.

Track with him as he pushes his way through the two hundred or so Headmasters who are standing around in the room, drinking tea and making genial and lively conversation. He nods pleasantly to various of them. Various snatches of conversation become distinct as First Headmaster passes.

SECOND HEADMASTER. The Old Boys' Association raised a quarter of a million in three months . . .

THIRD HEADMASTER. Our merchant bankers thought we could reckon on half a million . . .

FOURTH HEADMASTER. Our people suggested floating the school off . . .

FIFTH HEADMASTER. And we hope the school mosque will be finished in time for Ramadan . . .

SIXTH HEADMASTER. Only a couple of million, but we do have the same accountants as Mick Jagger . . .

SEVENTH HEADMASTER. So, anyway, an equerry came down and checked our security arrangements . . .

First Headmaster comes face to face with Eighth Headmaster.

FIRST HEADMASTER. Did you ring the school?

EIGHTH HEADMASTER. They say he left at ten.

FIRST HEADMASTER (*looks at his watch*). He said he was going to be here by three.

Mr Jolly pushes his way between them, smiling with embarrassment, discreetly searching.

MR JOLLY. I'm sorry — I'm just. I don't know whether.

FIRST HEADMASTER (*his eyes following Jolly*). Extraordinary appointments some governors are making these days. Or is that the state sector?

EIGHTH HEADMASTER. Chap over there came on a motor-cycle, by the look of it.

He nods to indicate where, and they both discreetly turn to look.

Pan to Mr Wisely, in his motor-cycling leathers. He is standing on his own at the edge of the room, holding a cup of tea and looking very uneasy. Mrs Wisely comes into frame, and speaks excitedly but inaudibly to her husband.

FIRST HEADMASTER. Good God, some *woman*.

Cut to First and Eighth Headmasters.

EIGHTH HEADMASTER. How did *she* get in?

FIRST HEADMASTER. Excuse me.

Pan with First Headmaster as he makes his way through the crowd to Mr and Mrs Wisely.

NINTH HEADMASTER (*to another Headmaster*). Then at Easter I'm taking the Classical Sixth to Jamaica . . .

FIRST HEADMASTER (*to the Wiselys, with great charm and courtesy*). Can I help you at all?

MRS WISELY. Where is she? Where's Laura?

FIRST HEADMASTER. I'm sorry?

MRS WISELY. Our daughter! (*Indicates Mr Wisely.*) He's going mad! He'll have one of his attacks!

First Headmaster glances at Mr Wisely, who creaks uneasily from foot to foot in his leathers.

FIRST HEADMASTER. Oh dear. Your daughter? Well, let's go and have a look for her, shall we?

He ushers them both towards the door, and speaks privately to Mr Wisely.

I'm so sorry. Someone should have explained to you — we don't bring wives and families.

MRS WISELY (*overhearing*). Wives? No! You bring eighteen-year-old girls doing their A-levels. I've never heard of anything like it!

FIRST HEADMASTER. Well, let's go outside and discuss it in peace.

MRS WISELY. Where is he? Where's Mr Stimpson?

FIRST HEADMASTER. Mr Stimpson? Ah, Mr Stimpson! Well . . .

But his eye has been caught by something out of view.

Excuse me one moment.

He turns to the Tenth Headmaster, who is the nearest.

TENTH HEADMASTER (*to another Headmaster*). Anyway, we're hoping the new solarium will give our sixth form a bit more appeal at the top end of the market.

FIRST HEADMASTER (*to Tenth Headmaster, indicating Mr and Mrs Wisely*). I'm so sorry! Would you show these good people into the room across the corridor?

TENTH HEADMASTER (*beaming*). Terrific! Delighted!

FIRST HEADMASTER. See that they both have some tea. (*To Mr and Mrs Wisely.*) I'll be with you in one moment.

Pan with him as he crosses the room to Gwenda, who is standing at the side of the room, surveying the Headmasters with a cold and bitter eye.

FIRST HEADMASTER. Can I help you?

GWENDA (*sourly*). I'm looking for Mr Stimpson.

FIRST HEADMASTER (*cheerfully*). We're *all* looking for Mr Stimpson! Come with me!

He begins to usher her towards the door. Pan with them as they go, and immediately find themselves next to Mrs Trellis, who is talking to a bemused Fourth Headmaster and a restless Mr Jolly.

MRS TRELLIS. So of course I told her. 'I don't *drink* sherry,' I said. 'I am a total abstainer, as you very well know. But I do not see why the glasses should go to Pam simply because she drinks . . .'

FIRST HEADMASTER (*to Mrs Trellis*). Let's give you a cup of tea next door!

GWENDA (*to Mrs Trellis*). I told you to stay in the car.

FIRST HEADMASTER (*to Mrs Trellis*). Oh, you're another of Mr Stimpson's party, are you? (*To Fourth Headmaster*

and Mr Jolly.) Pour them some tea, and take them into
the room across the corridor.

GWENDA (*to Mr Jolly*). What are *you* doing here?

MR JOLLY. Oh, I'm just. I'll fetch you a cup of.

*First Headmaster turns and comes face to face with Eighth
Headmaster again.*

FIRST HEADMASTER. He seems to have brought his entire
family!

EIGHTH HEADMASTER (*discreetly indicating*). Another one
here.

Mrs Wheel comes into frame.

FIRST HEADMASTER (*as charming as ever*). Let me guess!
You're looking for Mr Stimpson!

MRS WHEEL. I'm looking for the head doctor.

FIRST HEADMASTER. Ah. Let's see what we can find
outside.

He ushers her towards the door. They meet Mrs Way.

Mr Stimpson?

MRS WAY. Am I? (*Happily.*) I don't know *what* I am or
where I am!

FIRST HEADMASTER (*charmingly*). I know the feeling!

He takes her by the arm as well.

Cut to:

112. Interior. Corridor outside Common Room and TV Room. Day.

*Tenth Headmaster is just ushering Mr and Mrs Wisely into the
TV Room opposite the Common Room.*

TENTH HEADMASTER (*cheerfully*). Why don't you both
make yourselves comfortable in here, and I'll bring
Mr Stimpson over just as soon as I've found him. Terrible
bore, I know, but it is a private meeting.

*Fourth Headmaster comes into shot ushering Gwenda and
Mrs Trellis, both balancing teacups.*

MRS TRELLIS (*to Fourth Headmaster and Gwenda*). 'In fact',

I said, 'it would be an unfair temptation to her to put a sherry glass into her hands . . .'

TENTH HEADMASTER (*beaming welcomingly*). Mr Stimpson's party? In here, in here!

Cut to First Headmaster, arriving with Mrs Wheel and Mrs Way, also with teacups.

FIRST HEADMASTER (*cheerfully, to Tenth Headmaster*). Two more for you!

Pan with them as they reach Tenth Headmaster at the door of the TV Room.

TENTH HEADMASTER. Terrific! Super!

MRS WAY. Oh, this is the most exciting day!

Cut to two Plainclothes Detectives. They are approaching First Headmaster.

DET. SGT. RICE. Detective Sergeant Rice, Norwich CID. I believe you have a Mr Brian Stimpson here.

FIRST HEADMASTER. Nothing wrong, I hope?

DET. SGT. RICE. We'd just like a word with him, sir.

FIRST HEADMASTER. He hasn't arrived yet. We're waiting for him.

DET. SGT. RICE. We'll wait, too, then, if we may.

FIRST HEADMASTER. I'll bring you some tea.

He ushers them on towards the TV Room.

Cut to Tenth Headmaster, outside door of TV Room.

TENTH HEADMASTER. Stimpson supporters' club? In here!

The two Detectives come into frame, and Tenth Headmaster ushers them into the TV Room.

Do you take sugar?

Cut to door of Common Room.

Eighth Headmaster emerges anxiously. First Headmaster comes into frame.

FIRST HEADMASTER (*quietly*). Police looking for him now.

EIGHTH HEADMASTER. Oh no! Little boys?

FIRST HEADMASTER (*looks at his watch*). If he's *not* here by five . . .

EIGHTH HEADMASTER. I suppose one of us could say a few words . . .

FIRST HEADMASTER. I could have a go, if you like. Something about money, perhaps. Usually a reliable standby . . .

EIGHTH HEADMASTER. I hope he's not lying in some ditch.

FIRST HEADMASTER (*piously*). Absolutely.

Cut to:

113. Exterior. Roadside — Road (5) to Norwich. Day.

Close up of Stimpson lying as before. He is gazing reflectively up at the sky, talking quietly and intimately.

STIMPSON. It was going to be the start of so much, Laura! I was going to go into politics . . . I used to think: 'When I become Secretary of State for Education . . .' Yes! Don't laugh.

Pan to where Laura was sitting beside him before. She is no longer there. Continue the pan to the side of the road, where Laura is standing, out of earshot, hitching passing cars. She glances back at Stimpson, then concentrates on the cars again.

Cut to close up of Stimpson.

I thought I didn't mind. When I was in the monastery. I thought I'd resigned myself to it. But really I knew I'd still got time, you see . . .

Cut to Stimpson's point of view of the road-sign, upside down, and the drifting clouds in the sky above it.

Funny how you always know secretly when the last moment is. And when it's gone. And now it has . . .

Cut to close up of Stimpson.

. . . I mind, Laura! I mind!

Cut to Laura, standing beside the road. She thumbs a passing car. Its engine note drops suddenly. She turns to look.

Cut to open Porsche. It is just stopping, a hundred yards or so further up the road. The Driver, a middle-aged man in a sharp suit, who looks suspiciously like a shady motor-car salesman, turns round and looks back speculatively at Laura. The stop lights go out and the reversing lights come on.

Cut to Laura, at the roadside. She turns to where Mr Stimpson is lying.

LAURA. Mr Stimpson!

Cut to Stimpson, lying as before.

STIMPSON. Those clouds, though . . .

LAURA (*out of view*). Mr Stimpson!

STIMPSON. Perhaps I *could* just lie here . . .

He becomes aware that he has been called, and sits up.

Cut to point of view of Laura at the roadside.

LAURA (*to Stimpson*). Wait!

Pan with her as she runs along the roadside to meet the reversing Porsche. She bends and talks to the Driver. He nods, leans across to open the passenger's door, then turns back and faces front while he waits for her to get in. He does not see when she beckons urgently but discreetly to Stimpson.

Cut to Stimpson, on the ground, watching her. He gets up, reluctantly, pulling on his sandals, anguish returning to his expression. He groans, and begins to hobble towards the car.

Cut to Porsche. Laura is standing holding the passenger's door open, and trying to find the release catch for the front seat.

DRIVER. Come on, then, darling. What's the trouble?

LAURA. Does this seat tip up?

DRIVER. Don't worry about the car! It's brand new — it's only got twelve miles on the clock.

LAURA. What, you push this lever . . . ?

She pushes the lever, and the seat tips forward, just as

*Stimpson comes hobbling into shot. She bundles him into
the back seat.*

DRIVER. Hang about. What's all this?

*She tips the seat back, jumps in beside the Driver, and
closes the door.*

LAURA. We're together.

DRIVER (*stares at Stimpson's habit*). I don't believe this.

LAURA. He's got to get to Norwich.

DRIVER. I've seen them pull some stunts, but . . . a *monk*?

*Cut to Stimpson, in the back. No words come to him.
He gestures helplessly.*

*Cut to Driver and Laura. The Driver looks from Stimpson
to Laura. She gestures helplessly in her turn, unable to
think of any further explanation. The Driver turns to look
at Stimpson again. Suddenly he gives in, and gestures
helplessly in his turn.*

DRIVER. OK. A monk. What can I do?

He turns back to the steering wheel and lets the clutch in.

Cut to Exterior. Porsche.

It moves off and accelerates away up the road.

Cut to:

114. Interior. Porsche/Exterior. Road (5) to Norwich. Day.

Stimpson's point of view of Laura and Driver.

*Laura turns and sneaks Stimpson a brief little smile of
triumphant complicity.*

Cut to Stimpson. He looks away, appalled to be part of all this.

*Cut to Stimpson's point of view of Driver. He looks at
Stimpson in the mirror.*

DRIVER (*shouts over wind*). I'm surprised at you, though,
Father. Putting a bird out at the side of the road, hiding in
the ditch. Does your Father Superior know you travel
round like this?

*Cut to Stimpson. He looks away again, unable to meet the
Driver's eye. He realises that Laura is looking at him.*

*Cut to Stimpson's point of view of Laura. She has turned
round and is frankly grinning at Stimpson. She leans back
to shout to him privately.*

LAURA. Funny! You!

*She points at his habit, and turns back to face front. Then
another thought strikes her, and she turns round again.*

Speech! Like that?

*Cut to Stimpson. He moves his head from side to side,
acknowledging the painfulness of this prospect.*

*Cut to Stimpson's point of view of Driver. He looks in the
mirror at Stimpson.*

DRIVER. What?

Cut to Stimpson. He shakes his head wearily.

*Cut to Stimpson's point of view of Driver and Laura. She
indicates the Driver's suit to Stimpson with a little nod of
her head, then looks at Stimpson.*

Cut to Stimpson. He frowns, uncomprehending.

*Cut to Stimpson's point of view of Driver and Laura. She
discreetly repeats the suggestion.*

*Cut to Stimpson. He realises what she means, and shakes his
head decisively.*

*Cut to Stimpson's point of view of driver and Laura. The
Driver looks at Stimpson in the mirror.*

DRIVER. Frankly, Father, I'm shocked. You know that? I'm
not easily shocked, but I'm shocked.

LAURA (*to Driver*). Can we stop?

DRIVER. What?

LAURA. Stop a moment. By these trees.

Cut to:

115. Exterior. Wood — road (5) to Norwich. Day.

Pan with the Porsche as it stops at the side of the main road.

DRIVER (*to Laura*). What's the trouble?

LAURA. Go for a little walk.

DRIVER. Go for a walk?

LAURA. In the woods.

DRIVER. You? You want to go for a walk?

LAURA (*gets out of the car*). Don't you want to come?

> The Driver stares at her, then at Stimpson, then back at her, uncertain what to believe.

DRIVER. What, you mean . . . ? What?

LAURA (*nods at the woods*). No one around.

> The Driver looks at Stimpson, who looks away.

DRIVER. Well, this beats everything . . . Sorry about this, Father. Five minutes, that's all. Pick a few flowers . . .

> He gets out of the car and walks round to join Laura.

LAURA (*to Stimpson*). Come on, then.

DRIVER. Him?

STIMPSON. Oh, No!

> Laura presses the release and tips the passenger's seat forward.

DRIVER. You want *him* to come? You want Father there?

LAURA. Come on! The sun's out!

> She skips ahead of them, tauntingly.

DRIVER (*to Stimpson, confidentially*). Funny old world, isn't it?

> They follow her.

> Cut to:

116. Exterior. Clearing in woods — tree branch. Day.

Close up of squirrel. It is perched on the branches of a tree, watching something.

Cut to:

117. Exterior. Clearing in woods. Day.

Laura. She is standing in the clearing, gazing intently up at the squirrel.

Cut to Stimpson. He is standing some way off, looking uncertainly from Laura to the squirrel and back again.

Cut to Driver. He is standing some way off from both Laura and Stimpson, looking uncertainly back and forth from one to the other.

DRIVER. Look, I'll be frank. I'm out of my depth.

Cut to Laura. She is still watching the squirrel.

LAURA. We could take our clothes off.

Cut to:

118. Exterior. Clearing in woods — tree branch. Day.

Close up of squirrel. It turns and lollops away.

Cut to:

119. Exterior. Clearing in woods. Day.

Driver. He turns from Laura to Stimpson, not knowing what to think.

Cut to Stimpson. He turns his back in embarrassment.

Cut to Driver. He turns from Stimpson to Laura.

DRIVER. Go on, then.

Cut to Laura. She has turned to look at the Driver.

LAURA. You first.

Cut to Driver. He glances uneasily at Stimpson again, then back at Laura. He licks his lips, then suddenly takes the plunge. He rips off his tie.

Cut to Laura.

Go on.

Cut to Driver. He hesitates for a moment, then drops the tie on the ground and pulls off his jacket.

Cut to Laura.

Shoes.

Cut to Driver. He hesitates again, then slips off his shoes.

DRIVER (*firmly*). Now you.

Cut to Laura. She turns to Stimpson.

LAURA. Now Mr Stimpson!

Cut to Stimpson. His back is still turned, but you can tell that he has heard.

Cut to Driver, holding his shoes, and watching Stimpson.

DRIVER. Come on, then!

Cut to Stimpson. His back is still turned. He wriggles with reluctance.

Driver, holding his shoes and watching Stimpson. He has a sudden loss of confidence.

Oh, look, I'm not doing a solo . . .

He begins to put the shoes back on.

Cut to Laura. She looks anxiously from the Driver to Stimpson.

Cut to Stimpson, still standing with his back turned. In one sudden movement he drags the habit up and over his head, and stands there in his underclothes.

Cut to Laura. She turns from Stimpson to the Driver.

Cut to Driver. He stands looking at Stimpson for a moment, one shoe half on and one shoe off. He glances at Laura. Then he pulls the shoe off, tosses it aside, and starts to take off his trousers.

Cut to Laura. She is looking at the Driver. She turns towards Stimpson, and suddenly laughs with delight. Pan with her as she runs across to Stimpson, picks up the abandoned habit, and runs across to the Driver with it. He is just finishing taking off his shirt, and is reduced, like Stimpson, to his underclothes. Laura holds out the habit to him, smiling. He bursts out laughing at the idea. He tosses the shirt aside, and pulls on the habit. Laura collects up the Driver's abandoned garments, laughing. Pan with her as she takes them across to Stimpson. She makes him turn round and look at the Driver.

Cut to Driver, wearing the habit. He presses his hands together, and rolls his eyes up to heaven humorously.

Cut to Stimpson and Laura. Stimpson smiles uneasily at the

Driver's performance as Laura hands him the suit. Stimpson and Laura catch each other's eye. She jerks her head almost imperceptibly in the direction of the car. They turn from each other to look at the Driver. Then abruptly they turn back to each other and run, Stimpson carrying the suit.

Cut to Driver. For a moment he stands still in amazement. Then:

DRIVER. Hey!

He runs after them.

Cut to track with Stimpson and Laura as they flee through the wood. Laura is exultant, Stimpson terror-stricken and hobbling.

LAURA (*to Stimpson*). Key! Key! Find the key!

Cut to track with the Driver as he runs after them.

DRIVER (*shouts to himself*). I knew it! I knew it was a stunt as soon as he got in the car!

Cut to:

120. Exterior. Woods — road (5) to Norwich. Day.

Pan with Laura and Stimpson as they come running up to the parked Porsche. Stimpson is fumbling the car-key out of the suit pocket.

LAURA. Give it to me! Give it to me!

Cut to Pan with Driver, as he runs up to Stimpson to get into the passenger's door of the car.

DRIVER. Give me that suit! Three hundred quid that suit cost me!

He hurls himself upon Stimpson, beside himself with rage.

Cut to nearby tree. Back view of a Man who is standing peeing against the trunk of the tree. He turns his head and gazes open-mouthed at the sight of the raging monk.

Cut to Driver and Stimpson. The Driver is trying to drag the suit away from the terrified Stimpson. A sleeve comes away. A moment's pause, while Stimpson gazes at the sleeveless suit, and the Driver at the suitless sleeve.

You've torn it! Monk? *Monk*? You've torn the sleeve off a three-hundred-guinea suit!

A great roar as the engine starts. Driver and Stimpson both turn to look at Laura.

No! Not the car!

The Driver drops the sleeve and runs round to the front of the bonnet. Laura is struggling with the gear-shift.

LAURA (*to Stimpson*). Get in!

Stimpson picks up the sleeve and gets in to the passenger's seat.

Cut to Stimpson's point of view of the Driver. He is standing in front of the car, spreading his arms out as a human barricade.

DRIVER. It's not mine! It's a customer's! It's not insured!

Cut to Laura and Stimpson. She gets the gear in, and gazes forward with merciless determination. Stimpson covers his face with the suit. The engine roars.

Cut to nearby tree. The Man who was peeing has now turned round completely to face the scene, appalled. He is trying to do up his zip, but his hands move involuntarily out of dissuasion.

Cut to Porsche, with the Driver straddling in rage and terror in front of it.

No! No! No!

As he moves involuntarily backwards to absorb the expected impact, so the car roars wildly backwards away from him.

Cut to Laura. She brakes, and looks down at the gear-shift in surprise. She selects another gear.

Cut to pan with the Driver, as he gets his balance, and comes running forwards towards the car. He stops as the car, now evidently in forward gear, roars off past him.

Cut to nearby tree. The Man, still standing with his zip undone and his hands outstretched in pacification, turns from the departed car to the Driver.

Cut to Driver. He turns from the departed car to the Man

by the tree.

(*To the Man by the tree.*) I *knew* it! From the moment she stuck her thumb up!

Cut to Nearby tree. Not wishing to hold a conversation with a mad monk, the Man quickly collects himself and turns to go. He walks straight into the tree.

Cut to:

121. Exterior. Porsche/Exterior. Road (6) to Norwich. Day.

Laura is driving, exultant. Stimpson is sitting beside her, totally demoralised, struggling into the suit.

LAURA (*shouts over the wind*). You feel so good, though, don't you! You feel you can do anything! (*She glances at Stimpson.*) Don't worry. You can do 140 in these . . . ! (*She glances at Stimpson, who looks as wretched as before.*) Don't worry about the sleeve! We'll get some Sellotape! (*She glances at him again.*) We've got some money now! Feel in the pockets! How much have we got?

Stimpson reluctantly feels in the inside pocket of the suit, and brings out a wallet. It is stuffed with twenty-pound notes. The discovery does not gladden him.

LAURA. Oh, look, hundreds and hundreds. We could do anything! We could get Chinese takeaways! (*She looks back at the road ahead.*) I saw this film on television once. There was this bloke and this girl, and they went round everywhere in this car, robbing these banks and things. Did you see that, Mr Stimpson?

She turns to look at him. He gives a little inarticulate cry at something he can see ahead of the car. She looks ahead again.

Don't worry — I'll get you there . . . I'm a better driver than *her*, anyway . . .

Stimpson glances at his empty wrist. Laura notices.

We should have taken his watch as well . . . You know what's worrying *me*? The way I always seem to get involved with older men . . .

Stimpson gives her a sidelong glance of even greater alarm.

Cut to top shot of Porsche, as it does a suicidally racy overtake, forcing an oncoming car off the road.

Cut to:

122. Interior. Lecture hall — University of East Anglia. Day.

Close up of digital clock on the wall over the entrance doors at the back of the raked auditorium. It shows 16.56. Pan down and pull back to show the audience, some 200 Headmasters, chatting happily amongst themselves. Continue pulling back to find First and Eighth Headmasters standing at the front of the audience. They are turned round to look at the clock. They turn back, checking their watches.

EIGHTH HEADMASTER. No point in waiting beyond five, is there?

FIRST HEADMASTER. I'm going to talk about Charitable Status and Moral Leadership . . . Why can't he keep those damned women locked up?

Cut to Mrs Way. She is trying to squeeze past various Headmasters to an empty place she can see in the middle of a row.

MRS WAY (*to the Headmasters*). So kind of you. In everyone's way, as usual! I'll just sit myself down . . .

Eighth Headmaster comes into shot.

EIGHTH HEADMASTER (*almost as genial and courteous as ever*). Oh dear! Lost again, are we?

MRS WAY. Quite, quite lost!

Eighth Headmaster takes her arm and ushers her towards the doors at the back of the auditorium.

EIGHTH HEADMASTER. Let's see if we can find your friends.

MRS WAY. Oh, bless you, love!

Cut to:

123. Interior. Corridor outside Common Room and TV Room. Day.

Tenth Headmaster, looking increasingly harassed and dishevelled, and no longer genial or courteous, is at the open door of the TV Room, trying to persuade all the occupants of the room to remain inside.

TENTH HEADMASTER. Excuse me, but I am *not* shouting at you!

MRS WISELY. Excuse me, but you *are*!

TENTH HEADMASTER. Excuse me, but I am merely trying to get it into your head that *he is not here*!

DET. SGT. RICE. So when will he be here?

TENTH HEADMASTER. I don't know!

Eighth Headmaster ushers Mrs Way into shot.

MRS WAY (*delighted*). Oh, and here they all are, debating about which word to do!

EIGHTH HEADMASTER (*to Tenth Headmaster*). Can't you stop these people wandering into the hall?

TENTH HEADMASTER. No! I can't! They keep wanting to go to the loo!

GWENDA (*to Tenth Headmaster*) Mrs Wheel needs to go to the Ladies.

TENTH HEADMASTER (*to Eighth Headmaster*) You see? Then they don't come back!

He allows Mrs Wheel out.

MRS WHEEL (*to Tenth Headmaster*) Call yourself a doctor?

TENTH HEADMASTER (*to Eighth Headmaster*). Get me someone to escort them to the loo!

MRS WAY (*wanders off after Mrs Wheel*). Oh, off again, are we?

TENTH HEADMASTER (*to Mrs Way*). Not you! You've been!

He crams Mrs Way into the TV room. A Third and a Fourth Plain-clothes Detective come into shot from along the corridor.

DET. INSP. LAUNDRYMAN. Detective Inspector Laundryman, Regional Crime Squad.

EIGHTH HEADMASTER. Stimpson?

DET. INSP. LAUNDRYMAN. If I might have a few words with him.

TENTH HEADMASTER. In here.

*He ushers Laundryman and his Colleague into the TV Room.
They meet the first two Detectives in the doorway.*

DET. SGT. RICE (*to Laundryman*). Stimpson?

DET. INSP. LAUNDRYMAN. What are you doing here,
George?

DET. SGT. RICE. Stimpson.

DET. INSP. LAUNDRYMAN. Taking and driving and assault?

DET. SGT. RICE. No, taking and driving and kidnapping.

TENTH HEADMASTER. Right, inside then. Let's keep the
door closed.

He jams the door shut on everyone inside.

EIGHTH HEADMASTER (*to Tenth Headmaster*). Half the
police in England after him!

Cut to:

124. Interior. Lecture Hall. Day.

*A general buzz of conversation. Close up of First Headmaster,
at the front, tapping on the lectern.*

FIRST HEADMASTER. Gentlemen . . . If I might have your
attention . . .

The audience quietens down.

Thank you. Now, the time is . . .

*He looks up at the clock over the doors at the back of
the auditorium.*

Cut to clock. The time changes from 16.59 to 17.00.

Cut to First Headmaster.

. . . exactly five o'clock, and I'm afraid I have some bad
news for you. Our Chairman, Mr Stimpson . . .

*Cut to the doors, as they are flung open by Eighth and
Tenth Headmasters. Stimpson sweeps in, as grandly as if he
were in his own school hall, except that he is wearing the
Porsche Driver's suit, its sleeve reattached with sellotape, and
is followed inconspicuously but closely by a nervous Laura.*

Cut to First Headmaster, at the lectern.

(*Disconcerted.*) . . . is here!

Cut to pan with Stimpson as he comes down through the applauding audience, followed closely by Laura. First Headmaster gracefully cedes the lectern to him, then returns gallantly to place a chair for Laura. She keeps as close to Stimpson and as concealed by him as possible. Stimpson, facing the audience and acknowledging their applause with composure, does not see her.

Cut to Stimpson's point of view of audience applauding.

Cut to Laura. She slides her chair closer up behind Stimpson, very awkward and exposed.

Cut to Mr Jolly. He is sitting among the politely applauding Headmasters in the audience. He is not applauding. He is staring at Laura in agony.

Cut to Stimpson and Laura. He raises his hand for silence, entirely in control. The applause dies away. He lifts his eyes towards the clock at the back.

Cut to clock. It reads 17.00.

Cut to Stimpson and Laura. He lowers his eyes from the clock to the audience. Expectant silence.

STIMPSON. This is a historic moment. I stand before you today as your new Chairman — something that some of us never expected to see happen in our lifetime. We have come a long way together, to be where we are today.

He makes a gesture to show where they are today. It seems to include Laura as part of the 'we'. Laura glances up at him, surprised but pleased to be referred to, then lowers her eyes again, grinning with embarrassment.

Cut to some of the Headmasters. Their eyes go from Stimpson to Laura and back again. One of them turns to mumur something to his neighbour.

A long way . . . A long, long way . . .

Cut to Stimpson and Laura. He is slightly thrown by the murmur from the audience out of view.

And at this point I should perhaps explain that in the course of my journey I have become separated . . .

Cut to Mr Jolly. His eyes go back and forth between Stimpson and Laura.

Cut to Stimpson and Laura.

. . . separated from the text of my speech. I hope you will forgive me if I am a little disconnected.

He pulls his sleeve down unconsciously to set himself to rights, and the left sleeve becomes disconnected from the shoulder. An inch of shirt appears in the gap.

Cut to doors at the back. Eighth and Tenth Headmasters, standing just inside them, look at each other.

Cut to Stimpson and Laura. He automatically hoists the sleeve back into place, like a woman with a shoulder strap, and attempts to re-attach the Sellotape as he speaks.

Right. So I stand here today, if I may be personal for a moment, I stand here today, and I look out there, and what do I see?

He sees Mr Jolly.

Cut to Mr Jolly sitting among the Headmasters. He realises that Stimpson's disconcerted eye is upon him, and grins awkwardly. He makes various hopeless gestures.

Cut to Stimpson and Laura. She glances up at him, because he has stopped speaking, then follows his gaze to Mr Jolly. She draws back, disconcerted, and tries to hide even closer to Stimpson. Stimpson forces himself to take his eyes away from Mr Jolly.

I see myself. I see myself as I was then . . .

His eyes go back to Mr Jolly in spite of himself.

. . . an obscure master from an overawed comprehensive school.

He takes his eyes away from Mr Jolly, and looks with determination at the back of the hall.

Right. So what was I doing here?

Cut to doors at the back of the auditorium. They open, and Mrs Wisely enters and stands between Eighth and Tenth Headmasters, gazing accusingly at Stimpson. The doors swing to behind her, with their characteristic flim-flam.

Cut to Stimpson and Laura, both gazing at Mrs Wisely.

I was amazed to find herself . . .

Laura looks sharply up at Stimpson.

I was amazed to find myself invited to become one of your very select handful of Additional Women.

Cut to doors at the back. Tenth and Eighth Headmasters suddenly become aware that the cause of Stimpson's distraction is standing between them. They quickly usher Mrs Wisely out, letting the doors swing back flim-flam behind them.

Cut to various Headmasters. They turn to see who is making the noise with the doors.

Cut to Stimpson and Laura.

And I was even more amazed still at what I was listening to, because what I was listening to was . . .

The noise of the doors at the back again. He stops.

Cut to doors at the back. Mrs Wheel has just come in, and is looking round suspiciously.

Cut to Stimpson and Laura.

(*Patiently.*) Come in, then, if you're coming. No, because what I was listening to was . . .

The noise of the doors again. He stops.

Cut to doors at the back. Mrs Way has just entered, and is standing beside Mrs Wheel, looking round with a vague, benevolent smile.

Cut to Stimpson and Laura.

STIMPSON. Are there any more of you out there?

Cut to doors at the back. Mrs Way smilingly gestures that she will look. She goes out, letting the doors swing back behind her.

Cut to various Headmasters, turning to see what's going on at the back.

Cut to doors at the back. Mrs Way returns with Mrs Trellis. Flim-flam.

Cut to Stimpson and Laura.

STIMPSON (*still patient*). All right? Find yourselves
somewhere to sit . . . Right, so there I was, listening to the
headmasters of schools with great and glorious names . . .

The doors bang again. He stops.

*Cut to doors at the back. Tenth Headmaster has come in,
and is struggling to round up the three Old Ladies and
expel them.*

(*Out of view, suddenly losing patience*). Oh, sit *down!*

*Tenth Headmaster stops and turns to face Stimpson,
surprised.*

Cut to Stimpson and Laura.

Yes! We're all waiting for you!

*Cut to various Headmasters. They turn round again to see
who is being addressed like this.*

*Cut to Tenth Headmaster. He is staring at Stimpson in
amazement. He is going to explain, but then sees that
everyone is looking at him, and sits down instead.*

Cut to Stimpson and Laura.

Thank you. Right. So there I was, listening to the
headmasters of schools with great and glorious names as
they . . . kicked round a variety of weighty topics, as they
expatiated upon a variety of weighty balls.

A nervous laugh from somewhere.

I'm glad someone finds that funny.

*Cut to two Headmasters. One is whispering to the other a
comment upon Stimpson's performance. The other is
grinning.*

Cut to Stimpson and Laura.

There's no need to whisper.

*Cut to the two Headmasters. They look at Stimpson in
surprise.*

Cut to Stimpson and Laura.

STIMPSON (*genially*). Please — come up here and explain the
joke to the entire school. And who's that *creaking?*

Cut to the two Headmasters and others in the audience.

They look round to find the new culprit. Pan to Mr Wisely. He is creeping in, very careful not to let the doors bang, but with his motor-cycling leathers creaking at every step. He feels people's eyes upon him, and stops in embarrassment.

Cut to Stimpson and Laura. She bites her lip in sympathetic embarrassment, and glances up at Stimpson.

Come on! Come on! Let's get it over with. There's a seat down here, look.

Cut to Mr Wisely. He creaks to the seat indicated.

Cut to Stimpson and Laura. He watches Mr Wisely's progress.

Long way to Norwich, was it . . . ? Long way to that seat, too . . . Make yourself comfortable, then. Get all the creaking over . . . No rush . . . We've got all the time in the world . . . Time. Yes! Time! Right. Because I should like, before I pass on, before I pass on to other matters, to sound a note of warning . . .

Noise of the doors. He waits.

And still they come.

Cut to doors at the back. Mrs Wisely has just come in with Detective Sergeant Rice and the Second Detective. She is pointing Stimpson out to them.

(*Out of view.*) I was just talking, you might be interested to hear, about time.

Cut to Stimpson and Laura.

I was going on to say, I was intending to say, that time was the one thing we could all understand.

Cut to doors at the back. Mrs Wisely is still whispering vehemently but inaudibly to the two Detectives.

I was going to say we all understood that lateness was a discourtesy to others. But I'm beginning to wonder.

The two Detectives suddenly realise that all this is directed at them.

You're beginning to wonder, too, are you?

The Detectives sit down hurriedly. Mrs Wisely reluctantly follows suit.

Cut to Stimpson and Laura.

So perhaps the rest of us could turn round and face the front, and we'll all wonder together.

Cut to various Headmasters, who have turned round to see who was under attack. They hastily turn back and face the front.

Cut to Stimpson and Laura.

Right. Thank you. Because I'm starting to wonder if I'm the only person in the world who would be slightly surprised if the tide came wandering in half-an-hour after the lesson had started.

Noise of the doors.

Cut to doors at the back. Detective Inspector Laundryman and the Fourth Detective have come in, and are looking round the hall for the man they want to arrest.

Or if the sun came sauntering over the horizon at teatime . . . Slammed all the doors . . . Then stood there, gazing round the room, trying to find some chums to sit next to . . .

The two Detectives realise that they are the object of everyone's attention.

. . . while all the rest of us patiently wait to get on with the day's events . . .

The two Detectives sit down hurriedly.

Perhaps I sound a little old-fashioned. But imagine a spacecraft that was endlessly interrupted by latecomers and flapping doors.

Noise of doors. He looks anywhere in his impatience but at the back of the room.

It might just possibly go completely mad. It might just possibly lift off the launch-pad, and go screaming off into the depths of the universe, AND NEVER BE SEEN AGAIN UNTIL THE END OF TIME!

He looks at the back of the room.

Cut to doors at the back. Gwenda has just come in. She is staring like a basilisk at Stimpson.

Cut to various Headmasters. They turn to look at Gwenda. Then they turn back to look at Stimpson, with little anticipatory smiles, waiting to see her made an example of.

Cut to Stimpson and Laura. He is staring at Gwenda. He opens his mouth to say something, but closes it. Then he suddenly realises what Gwenda is looking at. He turns, and sees Laura for the first time. Laura looks up at him, and gives him a little conspiratorial smile. He looks back at Gwenda.

Cut to doors at the back. Gwenda compresses her lips ominously.

Cut to various Headmasters. They turn from Stimpson and Laura to Gwenda and back again. They are beginning to understand.

Cut to Stimpson and Laura. He turns to Laura, then to Mr Jolly.

Cut to Mr Jolly, sitting among the Headmasters. He is staring at Laura. He looks at Stimpson and discovers he is being stared at, and looks away hurriedly.

Cut to various Headmasters. They turn from Stimpson to Mr Jolly, then back to Stimpson. They have understood about Mr Jolly.

Cut to Stimpson, at the lectern. He turns from Mr Jolly to look at Laura, who looks away. Stimpson has begun to understand, too. He moves his arms away from his body slightly, in a gesture of defeat, and his left sleeve falls off. He closes his eyes for an instant, then opens them, and raises them long-sufferingly to the clock at the back of the room.

Cut to clock. It changes from 17.13 to 17.14.

Cut to Stimpson, at the lectern. The sight of the clock has got him back on the rails again.

STIMPSON (*matter-of-factly*). Right. Hymn 397. He who would valiant be.

He looks towards Mr Jolly.

Cut to Mr Jolly among the Headmasters. He is gazing at Laura. The Headmasters turn to look at him. He suddenly becomes aware of everyone's attention. He gets up, embarrassed. Pan with him as he squeezes his way out to get to the front.

Cut to Stimpson, at the lectern. He gestures for everyone to rise.

Cut to Audience. They rise, uncertainly but obediently, to their feet.

Cut to Stimpson, at the lectern. He waits. The sound of the audience getting to their feet dies away. Silence. He turns to look at Mr Jolly.

Cut to Mr Jolly, at the front of the audience. He is looking round desperately. There is no piano. He looks up at Stimpson pleadingly.

Cut to Stimpson, at the lectern. He gives up on Mr Jolly and turns back to the audience. His eye falls on First Headmaster, who is sitting near the front. He nods firmly at him.

Cut to First Headmaster among the other Headmasters. He glances round, but there is no escape. Very embarrassed and tuneless, he launches out into 'He who would valiant be.' Uncertainly and patchily the other Headmasters join in with him. The sound is confused still further by the fact that a woman's voice has joined in with the rest singing something else altogether, though what it is cannot be made out.

Cut to Stimpson and Laura. Pan with him as he makes a dignified departure, to the accompaniment of the hymn, through the auditorium to the doors at the back. The Headmasters, both those who are singing and those who are not, turn to follow him with their heads. But no one moves from his place.

Cut to Laundryman and the Fourth Detective. They watch spellbound as Stimpson flings the doors open and marches out, his head high. The doors close flim-flam behind him. Laundryman suddenly comes to life. He jerks his head at the Fourth Detective to follow him, and begins to move towards the doors at the back.

Cut to Laura, standing in her place on the platform. She throws off the spell as well.

LAURA. Mr Stimpson!

Holding out the sleeve, she runs after Stimpson.

*Cut to doors at the back. Laundryman and the Fourth
Detective are going out, followed by Detective Sergeant
Rice and the Second Detective. They are followed in their
turn by Laura, Gwenda and Mrs Wisely; First, Eighth and
Tenth Headmasters; Mr Wisely, Mrs Trellis and Mrs Wheel.*

*Cut to two Headmasters in the audience. They are turned
round to see what is going on, still thinly singing the hymn.
One turns to the other and indicates with a jerk of the head
that they should follow Stimpson out. Loosen to show the
whole audience, and the rush that the first two headmasters
have started. Half of them are struggling to get out of the
doors at the back; the rest are scrambling like school-boys
up on to seats and desks to see out of the windows. The
sound of the hymn crumbles away into the noise of excited
speculation and clambering feet. Go in on to the windows
at the back as various Headmasters climb up to look out
of them.*

Cut to:

125. Interior/Exterior. Lecture hall. Day.

*Beyond their heads, in the open air outside, can be seen two
parked police cars. Beside one of them stands Stimpson,
waiting in stunned and silent dignity to be arrested. The four
Detectives catch up with him, but before they can get the door
of the car open Gwenda, Laura, Mrs Wisely, Mrs Trellis,
Mrs Wheel, First, Eighth, and Tenth Headmasters have all
caught up with them, and begin shouting and arguing
inaudibly over Stimpson, wedging the door closed in the
process. Standing back and watching this scene are all the
Headmasters who rushed outside.*

Cut to:

126. Interior. Lecture Hall. Day.

*The Headmasters in the foreground, inside the windows, turn
to look at each other with pleasurable horror. As the noise of
voices and feet which replaced the hymn dies away, it becomes
clear that one voice is still singing. It is the dissenting woman's*

*voice that was half-audible before, and it is indeed not singing
'He who would valiant be.' The words 'This has been my
lovely day' become audible. One of the Headmasters in the
foreground turns to find the source of the sound. Pan in the
direction of his gaze to find the only two people still left
sitting in the hall — Mrs Way and Second Headmaster. She is
keeping him there with a gently restraining hand, and is
singing sweetly and happily the last few lines of the song to
him alone.*

MRS WAY. Just look at me and say
That you will remember too . . .

   Cut to:

127. Interior/Exterior. Lecture Hall. Day.

*Police cars and people outside, seen through windows as
before. The Police have now got the back door of the rear
car open. Tighten on Stimpson as he gets into the car, as
silent and dignified as ever, though still as sleeveless. Pan with
the two police cars as they pull away, pursued for a few steps
by Stimpson's frustrated victims. At the end of the drive the
first car turns left without stopping on to the main road. The
voice of Laundryman gradually becomes audible over the
preceding sound-track.*

LAUNDRYMAN (*voice over*). . . . also various charges relating
to the theft of certain items of gents' clothing, including an
ecclesiastical vestment, and of a wallet containing
approximately one thousand two hundred and thirty
pounds in cash. Do you wish to say anything? You are not
obliged to do so but whatever you say will be taken down
in writing and may be given in evidence.

STIMPSON (*firmly begins to make a statement that will
explain everything*). Right . . .

*The second car, the one that Stimpson got into, is beginning
to follow the first car to the left, but now swerves to the
right instead, then snakes wildly back to the left across the
whole width of the road.*

MRS WAY (*sings, out of view*).
. . . This was our lovely day.

The word 'lovely' is obliterated by a blast of offended

hooting, as the police car goes away out of frame to the left, and another car comes into frame from the left, forced off on to the verge. It stops, and the Driver jumps out, gazing after the departing police car. Fade the last note of the song into the background music as the shot fades into the end credits.